BEYOND THE FOOTLIGHTS

A History of Belfast Music Halls and Early Theatre

JIM McDOWELL

NONSUCH

Jim McDowell is a former primary school principal and a resident of Belfast. This book is dedicated to Nell, Nicola and Robert, Fiona and Alastair, Emma, Alexandra and Eve.

First published 2007

Nonsuch Publishing
73 Lower Leeson Street, Dublin 2, Ireland
www.nonsuch-publishing.com

© Jim McDowell, 2007

The right of Jim McDowell to be identified as the Author of this work has been asserted in accordance with the Copyrights, Designs and Patents Act 1988.

British Library Cataloguing in Publication Data.
A catalogue record for this book is available from the British Library.

ISBN 978 1 84588 570 0

Typesetting and origination by NPI Media Group
Printed in Great Britain

BEYOND THE
FOOTLIGHTS

Contents

Acknowledgements   6

Introduction   7

Belfast's Music Halls   9

Belfast's Early Theatres   81

The Great Outdoors   113

Extras   119

Bibliography   127

Acknowledgements

My special thanks to Mary Haegert and Pamela Madsen of the Houghton Library, Harvard University; the Chief Librarian and staff of the Belfast Central Library for their permission to use newspaper microfilm reproductions; Richard Anthony Baker; Donald Ker of Belfast Central Mission; the Reference Librarians of the Belfast Central Library Theatre Collection; the Reference Librarians of the Linenhall Library; the Reference staff of the Public Records Office of Northern Ireland, and my editor, Jenna.

Introduction

Some time ago I read that the Scottish comedian, singer and entertainer Harry Lauder made his professional debut at the tender age of sixteen here in Belfast. Looking for proof, curiosity led me to the newspaper library in search of that appearance. In my wildest dreams I had never imagined that this would lead to so much curious and interesting information about Belfast's former theatres and music halls.

While initially I had no luck with Lauder's first appearance, I found confirmation of the fact that following amateur experience in Scotland, he did make his first professional appearance in Belfast. In fact he began his career as an 'Irish' comedian at the Royal Alhambra on Monday 17 September 1894.

This started me off on a trail stretching across almost four centuries, from the 'plantation town' to the present-day city; between the bookends of the Sir Moses Cellars, where the tradition may well have begun prior to 1611, to the Grand Opera House, the last of our music halls still operating, and now newly extended.

Thinking about why I launched into this book in the first place, I've decided that my father and Uncle Frank must shoulder some of the responsibility. My father, no mean singer himself, and Uncle Frank, even better again, teamed up in the post-war years to perform such old chestnuts as *The Runaway Train, Susannah's a Funniful Man* and *The Bold Gendarmes* at socials and concerts.

Names of the music hall 'greats' were part of my childhood, as were their songs. Marie Lloyd, Florrie Forde, Albert Chevalier, Charles Coborn, Gertie Gitana, Harry Champion and Harry Lauder himself, lived on through their songs, sung around the piano in our front room at 68 University Avenue, barely interrupted by the trams that clanged past.

For years those memories lay stored away, only to be roused by the BBC's *Good Old Days*, its chairman Leonard Sachs, and the performers. When the series ended in 1983, over twenty years ago, the music hall age again faded away until I viewed a television clip of an old theatre being demolished and heard the comment that it had 'once been a music hall'.

It got me thinking about the Empire, the Royal Hippodrome and the Grand Opera House, as they were on my side of town. At that stage I didn't know about the Olympia Palace, which stood on the site of the Opera House in earlier years, or the Alexandra, later the Palladium, just around the corner at the Sandy Row-Grosvenor Road junction.

Appetite whetted, I began reading articles and books about music hall days across the water, before moving on to CDs of music hall stars and the songs that made them famous, and when I chanced upon the Harry Lauder reference it triggered my interest in Belfast's place in the scheme of things. I felt quite elated when I uncovered the all important advertisement that announced an outstanding career.

My search for Lauder's premiere revealed the names of the music hall legends and the names of the theatres and halls where they had performed. My scope widened as I found that I could not ignore the legitimate theatre and the greats who had visited it.

Seamlessly, I moved into social history. Unfamiliar street names from past centuries appeared, together with hotels, inns and taverns, where visitors might lodge or locals visit, to listen to the music on offer while enjoying a drink and a sing-song. Music was the magnet that drew people across the threshold. A glance at the *What's On* columns of today's local newspapers shows that little has changed.

Before I knew it, I had travelled back in time. I could see the alleyways and entries with their hotels and inns; I could sense the discomfort of the crowded, smoky, rowdy saloon bars—the intimacy they engendered and their threat of violence hidden just below the surface. Fanciful? Not when you've read newspaper columns of the time or walked down High Street, strolling by today's Crown Entry, Pottinger's Entry and Joy's Entry late at night.

A great distraction for me as I scrolled through endless microfilm was spotting a sensational 'breaking news' story sitting alongside some theatrical advertisement. In its early days, the *Belfast Newsletter* appeared each Tuesday and Friday. Its edition of Friday 9 July 1784 belatedly reports the death of 'Captain Cook on Sunday'. The paper informs us that 'Captain Bligh has arrived in London on 14 March 1790', and details his forty-eight-day epic voyage, covering 4,000 miles, before reaching Timor on 12 June, following the *Bounty* mutiny on 28 April 1789.

History came alive. First reports arrived of Clive's success in India, Wellington's at Waterloo, and of Wolfe at the Heights of Abraham at Quebec. I have to admit I enjoyed being sidetracked by exciting and important events such as these, as it was against this backdrop that the Belfast public went out to the popular theatre of the time. I could all but hear the buzz of conversation in the foyer, the circle, boxes or stalls, as Waterloo, Balaclava, and the American Civil War were being commented upon.

Now it is time to share what I have found. There will be some repetition of facts as I attempt to keep everything in-line. I have tried to give an overall picture of the entertainment scene across the centuries. It is our theatre heritage and it is undoubtedly incomplete. Almost all dates given have been verified by newspaper advertisements or by writings from the time.

However, I am confident that, while there may be omissions or oversights, I have unearthed all of Belfast's main venues, and corrected earlier factual mistakes along the way. (Those undertaking early research didn't have the benefit of microfilm; working with the original papers is laborious, and mistakes and incorrect assumptions are easy to make.)

I have included a chapter on the growth of the music hall worldwide, and have found that Belfast venues fit into this pattern.

Out of interest, I have included briefly a few observations on circus life in the city and a short list of some other entertainments.

There is so much more that could have been said about many other venues but space does not allow for it. I have also listed some of the books I have read or thumbed through. I like to think that what follows is a fresh look at our theatrical past and that it will make a contribution, and prompt you to look to those other books yourself.

I hope you enjoy the read!

Belfast's Music Halls

The Music Hall Era

This is probably the appropriate place to define what is meant by 'music hall'. Firstly, there is 'music hall', the place, and secondly 'music hall', the show; in other words, a venue as opposed to a performance.

To combine the two, the example to think of is *The Good Old Days*, which was screened by BBC Two from the Theatre of Varieties, Leeds, and last broadcast in 1983. The theatre played host to a variety show where olden-day acts were performed and the audience came dressed in period costume of the late nineteenth or early twentieth century.

Quite simply, the music hall performance was a professional variety show. Bills were up to twenty-seven, twenty-eight, even thirty acts at times, and I did see a copy of one thirty-four act string. Typically, there would be singers, musicians, jugglers, magicians, trapeze artists, comedians, ventriloquists, dancers, tumblers, and on and on and on. Such was the variety on offer in the third phase (1850-1950) of music hall.

Apparently the birthplace of music hall was Bolton, and in his highly informative *British Music Hall: An Illustrated History*, Richard Anthony Baker spells out this new development. As for the actual name 'music hall', this was first used at the Grapes Tavern in Southwark in London, after a singing room there was renamed a music hall in 1847.

Music hall's roots reached back to before 1650, but from that date, for a period of about one hundred years, the local inn or tavern was the focal point of entertainment for the working class. Artists sang, danced and played in competition with the drinkers, who were as noisy and uncontrolled as they wanted to be.

They were dreadful places—smoke-filled with regular brawls and fist-fights. Language was the deepest shade of blue, extremely crude, loud and raucous. Nevertheless, venues were packed and everything was fuelled by drink. There was a simple rule: if you didn't drink, then you didn't bother coming in.

This unruly behaviour continued well into the second phase of music hall (1750-1850), with loud singing an all-important ingredient as one group tried to outdo the other across the tavern floor. From this our pantomime tradition of left versus right, of upstairs against the stalls, emerged.

Records of these early days are sparse and while what I have is derived from descriptions from Britain, it would have been much the same here. Popular entertainment and the notion of people going out to enjoy themselves were becoming widespread. The working class went to the pubs; the aristocracy, as described by Samuel Pepys, was enjoying life in the Pleasure Gardens watching ballet, firework displays or vaudeville, or listening to concerts.

No matter who went where, and this holds true for the changes I am about to describe, the early scene was driven by food, drink and singing, in varying degrees of importance, and in an order determined by the patrons.

Notably absent is the middle class. There is no provision yet for those falling into that category, nor for the well-behaved upper working class; neither had a place to go. While the others went out to enjoy life to the full, these people remained at home, but that slowly changed as they made their feelings known. A century on something similar would happen again, when another milestone was reached.

To accommodate the 'left-outs', subtle changes were made over several years. The 'provinces' (everywhere outside of London) followed that lead. The middle class created a demand that had to be satisfied, and once the hostelry owners realised the potential for profit by catering for this new group, it was all change for many of them—though a lot of drinking clubs and places-to-be-avoided lingered on.

Furthermore, by around 1750 the appeal of the Pleasure Gardens was waning as their tone dropped. Now it was not only the respectable working and middle classes that needed to be catered for, but also the aristocracy, who found themselves at a loose end.

To satisfy this demand, a move to go upmarket took place and this was clearly visible in Belfast. It was satisfied either by building an annex to the existing premises or by the addition of an upper room. On occasion, an owner would try to make provision for the different social classes by creating several rooms, to gain the best of both worlds in the new marketplace.

What was to be called 'The Supper Room' came into being. Catch-and-Glee Clubs were formed where people met to sing and listen to music, this has remained central to the scene, as has the food and drink. Things became a little more restrained, for the proprietor was aware that people could vote with their feet. Having wooed and won the hearts-and-minds battle, he would go on to adapt still further in order to retain their custom.

It is important to note that in everything mentioned above, there are two main ingredients: atmosphere (crowded, rowdy, lewd, rude and smoke-filled, but alive to nth degree), and intimacy (jammed in, able to interact with your neighbours, close to the action). In later changes and expansions, both of these elements are lost, and comments are recorded to that effect, no matter what good those changes brought. The larger the new premises, the more distant the stage.

Artists wrote their own material and mainly performed their own songs—comical, bawdy or sentimental. Re-engagement depended on performance and it is important to remember that there were no microphones or sound systems. Quick-wittedness and a forceful personality were vital.

As will be shown, Belfast's music hall development owes much to two men in Britain. One was the forerunner of the music hall idea, and the other was known as the 'Father of the Halls', and he oversaw its early development as the year 1750 came and went.

Larger and larger supper rooms were being built and Evans's was the best in London. The family hotel, The Grand, opened in 1773 but in the 1820s the basement was developed, and W.C. Evans became chairman as 'Evans's Supper Room' took off. Change quickly followed and, in 1842, John 'Paddy' Greenmore took over and the music hall idea, as remembered by many, was launched. Affectionately known as Paddy Green (depending on where you were coming from!), he was about to set the standard for others to follow.

Evans's was in King Street, Covent Garden, and later became the National Sporting Club. W.C. Evans turned it into the place to be seen in and it was of the 'blue' variety, at a time when Catch-and-Glee Clubs, harmonic meetings and the coffee houses of the early 1880s were beginning to lose appeal. However, when Paddy Green stepped up, it moved off in a different direction.

Green built a new hall and, with a flair for innovation, he created a stage for the first time. It was unheard of, and he lined up top acts to grace it. The nobility, looking for something to take the place of the Pleasure Gardens, and combat the continuing decline in popularity of the Georgian tea rooms, coffee houses and old bohemian singing rooms, flocked to this new creation. Among his clientele in the 1860s were the Prince of Wales, a regular visitor, and Dickens and Thackeray.

Green vetted and then booked outstanding acts, all of which were male. Innovatively, he allowed ladies to attend, but once they had signed in they had to take their place behind a screen. His artists were paid a guinea a week, plus food. If Paddy Green was its forerunner, then it was Charles Morton who was rightly called 'the Father of the Music Hall'.

The third century of the music hall was about to begin, starting in 1849 when Charles Morton became landlord of the Canterbury Arms. He was a far-sighted businessman and, spotting a gap in the marketplace, demolished the building to replace it with the first purpose-built music hall—the Canterbury—which opened in 1852.

The Canterbury Music Hall had a stage, provided seating for 700 people, and ladies were admitted. Admission was 6d to the body of the music hall, which included refreshments. The gallery, fitted out with tables and serving food, cost 9d. He opened seven days a week and paid his stars between £30 and £40 per week. Morton's success soon galvanised others. Twice he improved the original Canterbury, bought new premises, and in London there was a starburst of theatres. Each city had several venues, and artists began to tour, with Belfast included in the circuit.

Music hall gained a place as a form of popular theatre alongside the opera, ballet or drama, and gradually the barriers faded; performers from the different styles of theatre began to interweave.

Professional entertainers went on stage overseen by a professional chairman, who, in the earlier days, was often the owner. He booked the acts, did the introductions, kept the audience in check and paid the performers. Singers were expected to include their latest 'hit', and the type of song fell into one of three categories—romantic, everyday, and humorous—with some merging of the topics. Attendance was huge and song subjects included anything and everything.

Songs like *I Have a Lassie* and *I'm Shy Mary Ellen, I'm Shy*, illustrate the romantic; everyday matters were well served by titles such as *The Football Match* and *The Village Pump*; while the comical and humorous elements featured, among thousands, such numbers as *If You Want to Know the Time Ask a Policeman*, or my personal favourite, *Nobody Loves a Fairy When She's Forty*.

The upmarket improvements were costly and, to make ends meet, the 'twice nightly' was introduced—two shows running back-to-back at 7 p.m. and 9 p.m. The stars moved around throughout the night, visiting different theatres. Rigid timetabling was required, with each act allocated a twenty-minute slot, which often had to be shared by more than one performer.

A close look at singer Whit Cunliffe's schedule is revealing and, like many, was either six or seven nights each week: The Chelsea Palace (7.10 p.m.), the Euston (7.45 p.m.), the Oxford (8.45 p.m.), the Chelsea Palace (9.45 p.m.) and the Euston (10.40 p.m.). By 1868 there were over five hundred music halls across the British Isles operating along these lines.

Performers came from all over the world and Morton signed up many. One such performer was Blondin, who made his professional debut at the Canterbury and, in 1896, performed in the grounds of the White Linen Hall, just before it was levelled. Again, Dickens and Thackeray were frequent visitors to the gallery, and Percy French was a regular star.

However, big trouble lay just beyond the horizon as the 1870s arrived. All was going well until 1875, when disaster struck, and Belfast did not escape. But before that, a digression, as the solution to the problem of what to do with the middle class was found.

The answer was the saloon bar, which was introduced in many of the premises that hadn't already been adapted. Rowdy elements were excluded from the saloon bar, which was a more dignified space, and were guided instead to the public bar.

The saloon bar was the halfway point between the rowdy, boisterous pub and the new large supper rooms and theatres. It was somewhere the respectable middle and working class could feel comfortable. The prime example, which almost everyone will know, is the Grecian Saloon, or Eagle Tavern, mentioned in this well-known rhyme, and it is the place where Marie Lloyd made her debut.

Marie Lloyd (Mander & Mitchenson, 1965).

Up and down the City Road
In and out the Eagle
That's the way the money goes
Pop! Goes the weasel.

Back now to 1875 and trouble abounded for the music hall. One after another they burst into flames. Their dry, wooden construction was an easy target for a knocked-out pipe or carelessly discarded match, and many went up in smoke. The year 1875 was so bad that it might well have been labelled the 'Year of the Infernos'. In 1873, Belfast's Alhambra suffered such a fate, as did the Theatre Royal in 1881. The situation became so serious that the London Metropolitan Board took action, introducing a Certificate of Suitability, licensing premises as fit to stage public amusement events. Overnight, hundreds of theatres closed, leaving many performers out of a job. Some found a temporary home in the pantomime theatre over Christmas, exposing them to a new audience who would eventually make their way to the replacement theatres, now they were aware of variety entertainment and its stars.

At this point a new era was beginning, and new financing from stock market companies poured in. Much thought and planning was given to the new buildings that were needed, and to the prospective new audiences. The transition from the smaller more intimate theatre to the larger venues was completed.

Stock market companies, investors and the new owners were aware that the new audiences would be vastly different. They would bring middle and upper class standards, so top designers and architects were employed to upgrade facilities to meet these higher expectations.

The new theatres or halls were luxurious and well appointed. Good lighting, comfortable seating, better sanitation and superb décor contributed to the sense of elegance. There were also tea bars on each of the four or five floors. These were imposing buildings with grandiose names. In Belfast there was the Theatre Royal and Grand Opera House, designed by Frank Matcham. The Palace, the Royal, the Empire, the Coliseum, the Alhambra, the Hippodrome, and the Palladium were all names to be found, not only here, but in most cities.

Music hall's heyday was in the 1890s. Street lighting was much improved and the new public transport system was operating, making it safer to go out at night, and the people did so in their thousands to see household names appear on stage.

These names attracted crowds wherever they went. Marie Lloyd (b.1870), Harry Lauder (b.1870), Bramsby Williams (b.1870), Charles Coborn (b.1852), Vesta Tilley (b.1874), Dan Leno (b.1860), Albert Chevalier (b.1863), Florrie Forde (b.1876), Harry Champion (b.1882), Sophie Tucker (b.1884) and dozens more top performers. Also around this time, those who were to become the first professional songwriters were being born.

The decline of music hall, paradoxically, began at the same time. The gramophone had been an expensive accessory until the 1890s, and some preferred to stay at home when this new form of entertainment became more affordable. On top of this came radio, although it must be said that those who heard the disembodied voices from the turntable and the airwaves were often attracted to the theatre to see those artists in the flesh. The scales were tipping against music hall though, and the silent movies, soon followed by the 'talkies', dealt further body blows to its popularity.

The First World War and the early influence of television finished it off as a major force, although such stars as Gracie Fields (b.1898) and George Formby Jnr (b.1904) gave it something of a boost. In spite of their contributions, and those of such artists as Arthur Askey, Ted Ray, Vic Oliver, Tommy Cooper, Elsie and Doris Waters, Two-Ton Tessie O'Shea, Morecambe and Wise and Sandy Powell, it was to be all downhill from here.

After the Second World War the decline was clearly marked. Cinema blossomed and offered a wide range of choice with regular programme changes. People simply stopped coming in the numbers needed to sustain the industry, and it was no different in Belfast to anywhere else.

The city fits comfortably into the picture painted above. The extent and variety of what was on offer here down through the years was amazing. No one theatre held exclusively to a particular form of entertainment.

The Theatre Royal leant towards the legitimate stage, while the Alhambra was almost entirely orientated towards variety. As for the others, all will be revealed shortly. Other entertainments, both indoors and out, ran along the traditional scene, and these will be discussed subsequently.

I wish that I could include all the strange and wonderful advertisements that kept the citizens of Belfast town and city and its environs entertained, but there are so many—but let us make a start, and step out onto the streets of Belfast some four hundred years ago.

The Beginning

Belfast's music hall development mirrored the pattern in Britain, and by the middle of the 1880s the saloon bar was emerging. As was the case across the water, the middle and upper working classes were looking for something better than food, drink, loud singing and unruly, quarrelsome behaviour. The saloon bar provided the answer. Singing saloons were to make their appearance.

Before referring in more detail to the Plough Hotel and its annexe, the New Harmonic Saloon, the Shakespeare and Theatre Tavern, the Burns Tavern and Concert Rooms among others, it is worth briefly repeating the facts that have led us to this point:

- There are records showing variety performances in the Market House.

- As the seventeenth century moves forward and on into the eighteenth, travellers gather in Belfast to journey by sea to North America, Europe, the mainland and further afield.

- Records show tourists visited the town in significant numbers in the mid-1600s.

- Inns, taverns and public houses were numerous, providing food, drink and somewhere to stay.

- There was an army barracks in Barrack Street, and a labour force extending the town.

- In 1574 the Earl of Essex reported directly to Queen Elizabeth I that the Brewhouse and Storehouse in Belfast were complete.

Bring all these facts together and the inescapable conclusion is that for the various hostelries there was a captive audience residing or going out for the evening in Belfast, needing to eat, drink and be entertained. This entertainment would be provided, if for no other reason than that it might well reduce the brawls and fist-fights that had become a feature of certain establishments.

I am quite confident that in the watering holes of the time there was a thriving entertainment culture. Belfast's early theatre scene was up and running, so it followed that the early music hall should thrive too. It is just not credible to imagine a tavern packed with soldiers, sailors, travellers, labourers and so on, supping ale without a sing-song, which would make a singer step up, and eventually lead to regular and organised entertainment.

Belfast drinking places begin to go upmarket in the early nineteenth century, with the aim of trying to create a more social and respectable environment for an evening out. One of the first to make a move was the Plough Hotel in Castle Lane, although sometimes advertised as being in Cornmarket. That matters little, however, for it definitely stands on the present site of the BHS store, where the Classic Cinema once stood.

The Plough was largely a commercial hotel, boasting that 'the larder is equal to the best in the United Kingdom' and that it had the largest coffee room in Belfast. It pledged that breakfast, lunches and suppers could be had at whatever time ordered. In the afternoon, visitors could have 'an ordinary … each day, at half past three and five o'clock'. Whatever that was! Perhaps afternoon tea?

It was to this seemingly first-class hotel, with very superior bedrooms and numerous sitting rooms, and the added luxury of 'warm and cold baths', that the proprietor Mr G. Davis added an early singing saloon. The New Harmonic Saloon was an annexe to his premises and first featured in an advertisement of 1832. George Davis continued to run the premises up to 1846.

Along Castle Lane at number twenty-one, another hotel was looking to improve its image. Situated on the opposite side, down at the corner with Arthur Street, was the Shakespeare Hotel. Just before this, it was the Theatre Tavern owned by James Stewart. It was appropriately named, for it not only served the casual customer, but the evening clientele en route to the Theatre Royal, with which the Shakespeare shared a dividing wall. Both of these were demolished in 1871 when the Theatre Royal expanded, sweeping round the corner from Arthur Street that September.

The 'Shakspeare' (its earliest spelling) had a thirty-year life, as a singing saloon in its earliest days and then as a music hall. It existed prior to 1841 but it was on that date that Thomas Frazer, the proprietor, made his move, perhaps prompted by the success of the Plough's New Harmonic Saloon.

During its lifetime it traded under five slightly different names, beginning with the Shakspeare, then the Shakespeare Concert Hotel, or the Shakespeare Concert Room during the 1850s and early '60s, until it finally adopted the Shakespeare Music Hall.

A fifth title was appended by Edward Prior Grey, who was twice its proprietor, for a few years starting in 1852, and for a second stint beginning in 1865, during which he gave it the name the Shakespeare Hotel and Tavern, but this was soon dropped.

However, the proprietor who should be remembered is Thomas Frazer, the original owner, who was determined to go upmarket. Frazer had other, grander ideas for his hotel, the Shakespeare. He decided to add on a singing saloon and recognised that he had to somehow attract a better class of audience. Unashamedly, he targeted this untapped market for, as far as theatre and music hall audiences went, it was a case of 'never the twain shall meet'.

Gradually performers were beginning to switch from one stage to the other and Frazer was about to try to persuade theatre audiences to do likewise, so he went for broke and, judging by the result, he obviously won.

Most singing saloons in the town had catered for the working class in the earlier years, but Frazer had other ideas, as we have seen. On Thursday 23 December 1841 he went next door to the theatre, having hired it 'for one night only' to promote the Shakspeare.

It was to be 'a grand concert' that would hopefully win over dyed-in-the-wool, generally upper class theatre goers. In his promotion of the evening he writes of 'having understood from numerous sources that a general desire exists among a number of respectable families to have an opportunity of hearing the performers whom he (Frazer) has engaged, begs to intimate, that in order to gratify those whom circumstances preclude from visiting his Room, he will be giving a Grand Miscellaneous Concert …'

'Respectable' families—of all classes—are who he is seeking out. Those who would not dream of attending the raucous, rowdy, brawling alehouses, but will now find somewhere more appealing to go.

At just this time, the 'snug' began to appear in a number of inns and taverns. It was a simple concept, and it was to appeal to members of the gentry who did not wish to lay themselves open to ridicule or abuse at the hands of a rough clientele. They could slip in and spend the evening in privacy, away from prying eyes. These snugs are still there in Belfast's Crown Bar.

Frazer makes no mention of a snug, but in his publicity he makes it known that his Concert Room, attached to the Shakspeare, is perfectly select, and is a place where gentlemen can depend on meeting 'none but the most respectable society', and it is for all those who 'feel a desire for musical entertainment'.

This advertisement is from 13 December 1842 and was one of a number seen in the year since the theatre's first promotion. It shows that things were working out for him. He had singers and instrumentalists, and a notable coup for this hall was securing the performance of the famous Scottish comedian Sam Cowell in 1850. Sam was a Belfast favourite, often appearing at Queen's Island and other centres. Although the Shakespeare was run by a Mr J. Watkins from around 1846, its burgeoning success was in no small measure due to the popularity of Cowell.

Once the title of music hall was taken, the bill read like a true variety music hall bill should: comedians, dancers, singers and contortionists appeared, with cancan dancers often a star attraction. Even ballet featured.

In fact, the Shakespeare epitomises the three stages of the music hall era—a pub that becomes a singing saloon, before moving on to become a music hall. Its final show appears to have been staged on 14 July 1870, after which it was knocked down to assist the expansion of the Theatre Royal.

One venue that did feature a snug was John Reids Burns Tavern. It was converted from the previous premises on the site in 1846 and stood at 8 Long Lane, just across from St Anne's Parish Church. The lane opened onto North Street, just opposite the place where the Deer's Head Imbibing Emporium still stands, exiting close to the Royal Alhambra.

Belfast Newsletter, 13 December 1842.

Its full title was the Burns Tavern and Concert Rooms, and gentlemen who ventured into town had their 'privacy guaranteed'. By 1858 it was no longer being listed in the *Belfast Street Directory*.

One saloon that didn't change its ways, and which typifies why such change was actually needed, was a singing saloon called Oddfellows Hall, a place with a dubious reputation. It was located at No. 5 St Anne's buildings, which ran from 22 Donegall Street through to 27 North Street.

The arcade opened in 1845/'46 which effectively dates Oddfellows. It was still to the fore in 1852 after which I lost track of it, and the next street directory lists a change of use. In 1847 a local newspaper correspondent describes it thus: 'Disreputable female vocalists who dared show their brazen and drunken faces before the very lowest audiences that could be collected in Belfast'.

No such accusations could be levelled at the Star Saloon. This was another of the early singing saloons and opened on 6 February 1852 at 21 Ann Street. This seems to be the date establishing its singing saloon days, although the first entry in the street directory of 1849 does point to an earlier existence under the publican Richard Kerr. It too followed the well-worn path—pub, singing saloon, music hall—though perhaps in a more circumscribed way than the Shakespeare, during its twenty-year lifespan.

Having found a *Belfast Newsletter* advertisement of Friday 6 February 1852, I searched painstakingly for others, but to no avail.

This advertisement read:

> 'Star' Concert Rooms
> 21 Ann Street, Belfast
>
> Mrs Kerr respectively informs the public that
> MR STEPHEN LOVITT
>
> The sterling comic vocalist
> Will make his appearance for the season in Belfast
> THIS EVENING
> Assisted by a talented company of vocal and other artists

The remainder of the advertisement lets us see that it was definitely a singing saloon with drinking facilities available, and for those who wanted privacy, a snug. It was well set up for a successful man.

> Wine, Spirits, Coffee, Cigars, etc., etc., of the best quality are available.

> Concert Room open every evening at half past five o'clock.
> A Private Snug for Gentlemen only.

Belfast Newsletter, 6 February 1852.

In 1863 Mrs Kerr was replaced by her daughter, Miss R. Kerr, who is now listed as the proprietor in the *Belfast Street Directory.* Her name disappears in 1865, however, when a Mr T. Gascoyne becomes the publican-proprietor.

Interestingly, in the 1868 *Directory,* Mrs Gascoyne is listed as the 'proprietress' but the name had changed to the Alhambra Concert Hall. This gives rise to the possibility that Dan Lowrey picked up on the name for his Royal Alhambra Theatre of Varieties, as in 1870 Mrs Gascoyne's Alhambra Concert Hall had certainly closed. Lowrey's Alhambra opened less than a year later.

He would not necessarily have poached it, or even been aware of it, as 'Alhambra' was a popular name for music halls and theatres of the time. The coincidence in this case, however, does seem to be rather large.

Victoria Square

Mention 'Victoria Square' and 'music hall' in the same breath and there will be many who quickly add 'the Empire'. For Nos 16-18 were indeed the home of what was arguably Belfast's most-loved theatre, or, to give it its full title, the Empire Theatre of Varieties.

The Empire opened on 3 December 1894 and closed on 3 June 1961, but it came right at the end of a chain of music halls that operated on the site, so, by way of introduction, and before I look at each link individually, a brief background to the area and those variety halls follows.

A century before the Empire opened, a private canal ran past where it would stand and, fifty years earlier again, the site had been a vacant lot. At the start of our music hall chain, several Colosseums worked under the address 16-18 Police Square. Prior to that it had been Poultry Square, so-called because of the market time.

Preceding the Colosseum era of the early 1860s was the Kitchen Bar (1859), just across Telfair Street. It became the official Empire Theatre Bar and was demolished in 2004 to allow work in the Victoria Centre to proceed. It has been relocated to a site further down the street.

Across the square stood Belfast's fourth town hall on the corner of Montgomery Street, where Cantrell and Cochrane's Mineral Water Company would be. Later, in 1871 up at the Victoria Street end and across it, the fifth town hall would rise, seemingly watchful of the goings-on outside the music hall doors.

A succession of music halls occupied the site and for a while the adverts read 'Colosseum! Colosseum!' Then it was 'New Colosseum' or 'New Colosseum Hotel' right through to around 1881. The story of the early Imperial Colosseum proves interesting and will follow shortly.

Thrown into the mix around 1879 there was a spell when it went by the name 'Traverse's Musical Lounge', but as we move through the 1880s the Empire that is still remembered by many is moving closer.

A new name follows the demise of the 'Coliseum' and in 1882 the 'Buffalo' appears and functions until about 1889. The Buffalo is followed in 1891 by the short-lived 'Bijou Empire' and the metamorphosis continues as the name becomes the 'Empire Theatre of Varieties'. This closes in autumn 1892.

And so to the real McCoy, which opened in December 1894 and turned out to be 'the (second) Empire Theatre of Varieties'. Now, starting with the Imperial Colosseum, we will take a look at those six or seven occupants of Nos 16-18 Victoria Square.

The Colosseum Era, the Buffalo & the Bijou Empire

Victoria Square was known as Police Square when the first music hall opened its doors there on the site where Belfast's Empire would stand. According to sources it was George Wallace's Imperial Colosseum. A.S. Moore claims it was 1865, while Alex Findlater, who will make the Belfast Empire famous, looks to 1861. 'George Wallace,' he says, 'built a small hall there which he called the Imperial Colosseum'. Neither claimant, in my view, is correct.

The first advertisement I could find was for Saturday 4 January 1873, run in the *Belfast Evening News*. No address is given but Wallace was both its lessee and manager.

Open every evening, with a powerful and varied company of star artistes. Doors open at 7; Concert at 7.30 sharp.

Then I turned up two advertisements, dated 12 May and 3 September 1873, giving the Imperial's location in High Street, but I failed to find the building in the street directories. Eventually, by sheer chance, I discovered it at 4 Orr's Entry, which opened out at 34 High Street, where in 1854 Mary Trevors ran the Wellington Arms.

By 1856 it was James Shearer's Saloon Bar and in 1858 Edward Shearer was in control of the Colosseum Concert Tavern, aka the Colosseum Concert Hall (1865/66).

Continuing the search of street directories revealed that Mrs Shearer had reinvented it as the Imperial Colosseum, with George Wallace emerging to control it in 1873. So when did he arrive in Police Square?

It seems to have been at the beginning of 1875, for the *Belfast Newsletter* advertisement of 28 February shows him in control of his Imperial Colosseum. Occasionally concerts featured but the majority of acts were variety.

Wallace was a song-and-dance man and a publican who established the Imperial, first as a singing saloon, not on the 14-16 site, but at No. 18. The directories show that No. 14-16 was occupied in 1861 by Hugh McClelland, flax merchant; in 1868 by a wine merchant; in 1870-1877 by W. Lowe, a spirit dealer and cement merchant. Given this, I'm not sure as to what Moore and Findlater were referring. Wallace eventually sells out to Lindon Travers who had been a support act in February 1875.

Strangely, although the actual address of the Imperial Colosseum is given in early advertisements, such as those from 12 May and 3 September, as being High Street; one person whose family should know the truth was Alex Findlater, the man responsible for financing the Empire itself. For his book he must surely have drawn on previous theatre records available to his family when the Empire purchase was made. In *Findlater – The Story of a Dublin Merchant, 1774 – 2001*, he tells us that 'George Wallace in 1861 built a small hall on the site of what would become the Empire, which he called the "Imperial Colosseum"'. Yet another date is then thrown into the arena. Again I could find no evidence, but most advertising was done through the distribution of hand bills.

The programme was varied; sometimes a concert evening, but more commonly pure variety. The bill of 28 February 1873 is a good example and included: Miss Theresa Parker, soprano; Mr Peter Aiken, the eminent comic; Marriot's Unequalled Troupe of American Minstrels; and half a dozen other acts.

Among them was 'Lindon Travers—the Great Baritone', who would become involved in the building's management, and who worked hard to improve its status as the population continued to grow. Colosseum remained as part of the title for some years before Travers brought about a change. For a time it was the 'New Colosseum Hotel', before it reverted to 'New Colosseum' for a period. These titles stretched through to around November 1881, with a break only when Travers was in control.

By 1879, Lindon Travers was in management and was providing wide-ranging variety in the best music hall tradition: jugglers, mimics, dancers, singers, comedians, comic vocalists, and all the while he was performing, accompanied by his wife. His determination brought about a name change to 'Travers Musical Lounge', before he chose one of the previous names: 'The New Colosseum, Select Musical Lounge'. He then changed the title again, to 'Travers Musical Theatre'—but what's in a name?

Belfast audiences resisted change, and it was not, after all, the name that was the problem. It was simply that the building was too small. The name changes hadn't increased popularity, and the discouraged Travers threw in the towel, apparently selling to a Mrs Sanders, whose name features in the advertisements, headed 'New Colosseum Hotel'. Travers himself was still appearing on stage. On 24 September 1879 he had claimed the 'Extraordinary success of this favourite musical lounge', but his handover to Mrs Sanders was just around the corner.

At this point the admission was still 6d or 1 shilling, but now the 6d ticket included refreshments. Mrs Sanders, however, stated that admission was free, but 'refreshments of the best quality at a moderate tariff' were available. Her new Colosseum was also a select musical lounge, with a billiards room and bar, open daily. What is interesting is the main point in her advertisement of 10 May 1881:

This elegant and commodious musical lounge now open for the Summer Season for Select Harmonic Meetings (for Gentlemen only), when the best Professional and Amateur Talent will appear. Concert commences at Eight.

Above left: Belfast Newsletter, 4 January 1873.

Above right: Belfast Newsletter, 3 January 1880.

Things went 'pear-shaped' for the proprietress on 14 November 1881 when the following appeared in the press:

> Owing to the Temporary Suspension of License, and pending the Appeal in the Court of the Queen's Bench, the above hall will remain open on Temporary Principles pro tem.

Shortly after, it disappears from the amusement columns as the journey towards the Empire continues. Lindon Travers had hoped to create his musical lounge as a place where the performers and the public could meet, mix and enjoy refreshments. It didn't work for him, nor did it work for Mrs Sanders. She too failed because of its small size. Alex Findlater writes that what we would describe as a makeover took place before it opened as the Buffalo, which proved reasonably successful for the new man in the hot seat, Mr E.W. Patrick (a.k.a. E.W. Partrick).

Belfast Newsletter, 10 May 1881.

While there is some doubt about the exact date of the closure of the Colosseum, there is none surrounding the opening of its successor, although the spelling of the proprietor's name varies from Partrick to Patrick and back again. Then, twelve years later, when working at the Empire's opening night (12 March 1894), I spotted E. W. Partrick, stage manager of the new building.

On 9 December 1882, the *Belfast Morning News* signals the opening of the Buffalo Variety Theatre and stated, '(Late Colosseum): Proprietor E.W. Patrick'. The advertisement, repeated over the next fortnight, reads:

The above Hall, having undergone a thorough restoration, cleansing, and re-decorating, will open at Xmas, with a carefully selected variety company.

The Bar and Billiard Room now open daily.

On Saturday 23 December 1882 it gives details of the artists, and the admission is 6d and 8d.

On Christmas Day, Monday 25 December, it opens at 2 p.m. and 6 p.m., Thursday (Boxing Day) and Saturday 2 p.m. and 7 p.m., other evenings 7 p.m., with powerful company: N.C. Bostock-Comic King; Maggie Latour-Guitarist; Grace Harold-Male Impersonator; Felix Rosen-Pianist; etc. The rest of the list that follows is typical music hall fare.

E.W. Patrick had engaged Belfast architect Vincent Craig to remodel the building and continued with the 'free-and-easy' style of the previous owners. Like Travers, and similar establishments across the water, he hoped that this approach would succeed. The advertisers pointed out that the Buffalo was 'one minute from The Theatre'. It had become a singing saloon with an annex where 'the well-to-do could avoid the abuse of the gallery'. (J. Gray)

Belfast Newsletter, 14 December 1882.

The intention of both, and probably also Mrs Sanders in her hotel, was that audiences and performers would mix and mingle in the bar area. However, even his inducement of a free bottle of stout included in the twopence admission was not enough to ensure the survival of his vision.

The format changed and shows continued until Wednesday 27 February 1889, after which I could find no further advertisements. Over the years there were the usual turns, but some of the more unusual descriptions are worth recording. Like so many of the other proprietors, Patrick was regularly on stage and alongside him on occasions were:

Ben Taylor-The One-Legged Prize Packet Novelty,
Miss Annie D'Laura-Dancer in a *Real Looking Glass*,
Mr & Mrs Pat Langag-Champion Top Boot Dancers of the World,
La Petit Engell-Juvenile Prodigy,
Last Six Fights of Miss Emily Lovely-Serio Comic Vocalist.

All this and much more could be viewed from the pit or gallery for sixpence and, depending on the particular show, eight or ninepence for the relative comfort of the orchestra stalls.

In 1892 Patrick emerged as proprietor of a new music hall, not too far from the Buffalo. In theatrical terms, the Buffalo Theatre went 'dark' following its closure at the end of February 1889. Trawling microfilm is 'a bit hit and miss'. If the Buffalo did continue longer, I was unable to score a hit. The first Bijou strike I made was in the *Belfast Telegraph* of 5 December 1891, as yet another name emerged.

The Saturday evening paper's amusement column read:

Bijou Empire

The above hall will positively open Monday next, December 7th with a first-class company.
For particulars see Bill and future advertisements.
General Manager – John J. Stamford

John J. had been a former manager to Willie Ashcroft at the Alhambra, and now took his turn to parade variety. The interesting thing at this point in the Empire's history is that the proprietors of the Bijou are named as 'The Empire Music Hall Company Limited'. Its opening night advertisement reads:

The above Handsome Variety Theatre will open its doors to the public on Monday
December 7th, 1891 and every evening during the week. Matinee every Saturday.
Doors open 2.30, performance at 3.

Curiously, no time is given for evening curtain-up although subsequent performances chiefly start at 7.45 p.m. Price of admission ranged from balcony and lounge at 1s 6d, pit stalls 1s, and gallery 6d. It is pointed out that there is 'No Free List' (press excepted). Certainly the management appear to have pushed the boat out for opening night. Some featured acts were:

The Chicago Trio-American Speciality Team, on their first visit to Ireland
The Two Koroskos-Single & Double Japanese Jugglers
Mr J. E. Cheevers-Our Old and Tried Favourite Comedian and Dancer
Miss Anne Brighstain-Refined Serio-Comic Vocalist

These and others all came from theatres in London, Paris and beyond. After this opening week, things returned to normal. Hypnotists, jugglers, singers and dancers continued to visit and prices evened out at 6d, 9d and one shilling.

John J. Stamford remained as general manager and saw it close on 16 January 1892. When next his name appears, it is as manager of the Empire Theatre of Varieties, Victoria Square, Belfast on 6 September 1892, as listed in a newspaper advertisement. It is a short-lived venture, as the last advertisement is on 6 October 1892. Subsequent to that nothing can be found for two years.

The Empire Theatre of Varieties

The opening night at the Empire Theatre of Varieties was the equivalent of today's red-carpet premiere. On Monday 3 December 1894 a huge crowd gathered outside, hoping against hope for a ticket, but with a special excursion train bringing three hundred invited guests from Dublin and a continuous stream of theatre goers, there was none to be had for the Victoria Square hopefuls. The Dublin guests arrived at midday and returned home after the show, having been entertained in a city hotel.

The cast list was impressive and, just as in London and other cities on similar occasions, the middle classes and gentry were well represented in the new, upmarket theatre, with the opening night proving a huge success. There were rave reviews from the local press. 'A brilliant success' claimed the *Irish Times*; 'A brilliant opening' said the *Northern Wing*, while the *Belfast Telegraph* described the interior as a 'marvel of Moorish magnificence'.

Right: Opening night, advertised on Monday 7 December 1891.

Below: Belfast Morning News, Thursday 6 October 1892.

The owner was Adam Findlater, whose family would maintain their connection with the theatre for years to come. His manager was Dan (Daniel) Lowrey, son of the Alhambra's Dan Lowry. Before moving on, a brief look at the history of the site is needed, to see how this situation came about.

Both men were Dubliners and had a proven theatre track record. Findlater was looking for an opportunity to establish a theatre in Belfast. He was aware of the current situation and that while the Colosseums, the Buffalo, the Bijou Empire and the First Belfast Empire Theatre of Varieties had struggled, the real problem was that of size. As change of name followed change of name, and attempted improvements followed the previous alteration, Findlater moved to take over John J. Stamford's Empire Theatre and began an immediate and complete rebuilding. His aim was to run it alongside the Star Theatre of Varieties in Dublin. Those in control at the Empire hadn't the financial resources to achieve their goal and were bought out by Findlater, who had the financial know-how, raising the money after a Dublin flotation of £1 shares—today's equivalent would be approximately £80.

On the evening of Saturday 1 December, the *Telegraph's* preview was glowing in its praise, describing it as, 'a notable addition to the amusements of the city' and 'the realisation of a mature design'. It went on:

> … the bulk of the upholstery was an attractive sage colour with the exception of the five tableau curtain and proscenium hangings, which were figures silk brocatelle in two shades of gold. Castle bevelled mirrors were placed at effective points and electricity had been adopted at the lighting agent … The general effect of ornamentation is too gorgeous for verbal description.

It is said to have been fireproof throughout and 'superbly finished and tinted in cream and two shades of gold'. Entertainment promised 'without exception the mightiest combination of variety talent ever seen in Ireland'.

Dan Lowrey Jnr was in charge and he went on a charm offensive to promote the new building prior to its December opening. He organised two-hour private tours of the new theatre for some three hundred of those involved in the professional and commercial life of the city, who were well entertained, as 'befitted those of the ruling classes'.

Across the water, it was fashionable for women to attend theatres and music halls, so why not the Empire, he reasoned. His lavishly styled interior overcame any possible resistance of the business community and middle class. Hard work and more promotion brought about a situation in which, for the first time in Belfast, women could attend a venue of this kind 'without reproach'. Meanwhile, the *Belfast Evening Telegraph* of Monday 3 December 1894 read:

Empire Theatre of Varieties
To-Night   To-Night
The Grand Opening
Will take place

THIS MONDAY EVENING
3rd December
Gigantic Inaugural Company
A Perfect Shower of London Stars
Production Without Parallel
In The History Of The Variety Stage In Ireland
Replete With Variety Gems

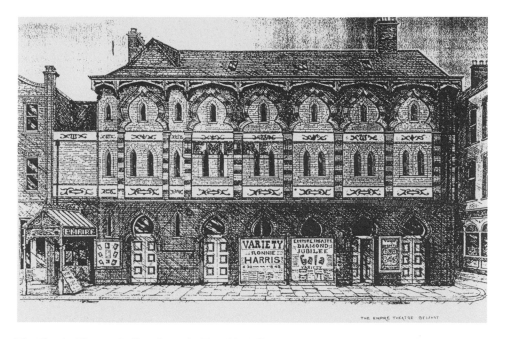

The Empire Theatre, Belfast, drawn by Tom McNally.

And chief among them were Little Tich, from the great London Halls—a comedian, popular on the European continent and America, renowned for his eccentric dancing in long-footed boots; Chirgwin, world-renowned for his role as 'the white-eyed Kaffir'; Miss Lucy Clarke, the Welsh nightingale, a gold medallist at the Royal Academy of Music; and neither last nor least, The Fred Karno Troupe. Fred Karno was an impresario who put together the complete show. Anyone working for Karno was made for life as he employed only the very top artists. Jugglers, singers, dancers, comedians, acrobats, and musicians all hoped for Karno's approval.

At first Karno had only just the one touring troupe, but as it proved itself to be top-class entertainment, others were added, until there were five on the road. One of these was always a regular in Belfast. Among the comedians was Robb Wilton, whose catchphrase brought a smile to those who listened to him on the wireless during the war years: 'The day war broke out, my wife said to me, "Well, what are you going to do about it?"'

However, by far Karno's greatest catches were those who would dominate the world stage and continue to entertain us on film today, for it was Karno who introduced audiences to Charlie Chaplin and Stan Laurel.

Chaplin was his lead for the many variety sketches and proved an instant success, and it was he who gave Stanley his big break. Chaplin, strangely, refused the lead role in yet another new sketch and pointed Laurel out to Karno in 1908. 'He is the one you need for this one,' he said, and the rest is history. He must have enjoyed his visits here, because when the theatre celebrated the Diamond Jubilee of its opening he sent a telegram offering his best wishes to everyone, along with 'long years of peace, prosperity and happiness'.

Charlie Chaplin had already been here several times in 1906 and 1907 and lodged with Mrs Jane O'Neill in 24 Joy Street opposite the school, and again in 1909. He was even here in May 1905 when he performed in the Royal Alhambra as one of the 'Eight Lancashire Lads', a song-and-dance troupe. He was, quite literally, following in his father's footsteps, as his father had been here in 1889.

Left: *Belfast Telegraph*, 6 June 1934.

Middle: 22 June 1896. Courtesy of the Belfast Central Library Theatre Collection.

Right: 15 June 1896. Courtesy of the Belfast Central Library Theatre Collection.

The Georgian terrace remains today. All that is missing is a blue plaque recording the fact on this beautifully restored house in the terrace just off May Street. His granddaughter still lives in the city today.

It was a straight walk down to the Empire for Chaplin, and I have often wondered if Stan Laurel accompanied him. I can offer only circumstantial evidence that Laurel was here sometime between 1906 and 1909, and that his visit to the Grand Opera House in 1952, with Oliver Hardy, was his second to the city.

Karno's troupe visited regularly after Laurel was promoted and we know that prior to that promotion he was Charlie's stand-in, and toured with him. They struck up a firm friendship and when they landed in America they even shared a room, as they had done when touring at home. Chaplin was just twenty years old at this stage.

All this is impossible to prove but I have convinced myself that it happened. Karno's troupe visited often in 1908 and 1909. Chaplin starred several times. Laurel was his stand-in. For me, it is a nice thought even if I am wrong. I'm sure someone out there has that programme hidden in their attic and can help me prove it one way or the other.

While all this seems a bit of a digression, it is also a final acknowledgement to Karno, whose entertainers played in not only the Empire but the Grand Opera House, the Alhambra and the Royal Hippodrome for the troops of the First World War. He was known the length and breadth of the British Isles and when the soldiers found themselves in the trenches, one penned the following verse, which helped transport them back home and to better times, and elevated Karno to folk-hero status. It is sung to the hymn tune of *The Church is One Foundation*.

> We are Fred Karno's army
> A jolly lot are we
> Fred Karno is our Captain
> Charles Chaplin our O.C.
> The Kaiser he will say-ay
> Hoch! Hoch! Mein Gott
> What a jolly fine lot are
> The boys of company A (or B or C)

Karno—wire-walker, juggler, gymnast, mandolin player—eventually ran over thirty troupes worldwide and introduced the custard-pie-in-the-face routine. From his routines, the Keystone Cops evolved.

Now back to the Empire, where the audience were waiting for a full fourteen-piece orchestra to stop playing and allow the show to start. In their programme they can read about the stars mentioned earlier. Some of the Dublin visitors, or even the Belfast people, may have bought shares in the flotation at one pound each.

This was a gala night and it was a great success. There was a range of prices for those who paid. A private box cost one guinea (£1.10), equivalent to approximately £90; cheaper boxes cost 75p to us but 15 shillings back then, or approximately £60. For anyone seated in a numbered reserved seat it was half a crown or £10, and that was in the stalls. Admission to the promenade and stalls was 1 shilling (5p) or £4, while the gallery was sixpence or £2. A good time certainly seems to have been had by all!

There was just one snag in all the euphoria surrounding the opening of the new theatre, which would certainly play its part in Dan Lowrey losing his job and Adam Findlater losing more than a few nights' sleep. Unbelievably, the sight lines were so bad that from large areas of the theatre it was impossible to see much of the stage. Boxes along the sides ran in straight lines. This was a major problem for Findlater, for as the *Belfast Telegraph's* journalist wrote, tongue-in-cheek, 'it is nevertheless a fact that when people go to a place of entertainment … they have the right to see a performance.'

The financier recognised immediately that tinkering with the interior was not an option. After taking specialist theatrical advice, Findlater and Lowrey bit the bullet, pulled the theatre down and started again. This time they got it right and the Empire, which the *Belfast Telegraph* commented on as having entertained us for a few short weeks, was magnificently rebuilt and opened on 26 October 1895 as a completely new building—but unfortunately it was still flawed.

Another nail in Dan Lowrey's managerial coffin at the Empire was driven in when he was forced to admit that he had misread the plans and that the accommodation was not for over 2,000 people, but for around 1,100. So in 1897 he had to resign. However, before that there was a problem in January 1896, when a fire destroyed the dressing room and engine room, but Lowrey organised a benefit for the artists who had lost their costumes. The £60 raised may seem paltry, but today it would be the equivalent of almost £5,000.

Once the Empire opened again, Lowrey was buffeted by another storm. Respectability was of the utmost importance in polite society. There were complaints about the quality of the entertainment being offered and newspaper reports of 'occasional rowdyism' did not help.

One such report read, 'the audience's behaviour interrupted and interfered in a manner that reflected the utmost discredit upon one part of the house'. A stinging rebuke such as this, and there were others, led to a further slump in attendance and financing. Action was needed to reverse matters but it wouldn't be undertaken by Lowrey.

Dan Lowrey, along with Findlater, still had an ace to play and it was to be an historic occasion at the Empire. It had begun in Paris a year earlier, in 1895, and had already taken place in Dublin a month or so previously.

In the French capital, the Lumière brothers had been working at creating moving pictures and, at a show in 1895, were putting on their first cinematography showing.

On its first day of showing there was such a poor response by the public that they faced bankruptcy. As a last resort they installed a movie camera outside and promised passersby that if they returned the next day, they could see themselves in the moving pictures.

The stunt worked and from then on the cinema was packed and the worldwide launch of moving pictures was ensured. Faced with a similar lack of interest at its opening in 1935, the Strand cinema in Holywood Road used an almost identical ploy, while just over thirty years later the Empire staged another premiere. Ireland's first radio-theatre broadcast was transmitted in 1927.

Belfast had its own film-maker and he was just beaten to the draw by the French connection. Professor Kineto did much to increase the popularity of early cinematography, producing films with a local interest, and one enterprise in particular had a direct Empire connection.

When Queen Victoria visited Dublin in April 1900, Kineto shot some footage, returned by train, processed it in Belfast and showed it to the packed-out Empire at 10 p.m. that evening. Professor Kineto derived his name from the American Kinetoscope, or Edison's Kinetoscope, for he was actually a Belfast photographer called J. Walker Hicks, whose films were shown regularly at the Empire.

The Empire's advertisement for Monday 16 November 1896 reads:

TONIGHT   TONIGHT

The Sensation of Europe

Londons Rage   Dublins Rage

The Marvellous, Perplexing and Original

LUMIÈRE CINEMATOGRAPHE

(From the Empire Theatre London)

This was followed by a list of the music hall times for the evening.

What exactly was it that the audience flocked to see? A minute-long screening entitled *The Arrival of a Train*. Fifty feet in length, it began with a railway line stretching into the distance, along which a railway engine races towards the audience and draws to a halt. The passengers alight and walk off-screen past the cameras. It had the Empire audience on its feet applauding. Several other minute-long films were shown to add to the excitement. No admission prices are given in the advertisement and five weeks later the Grand Opera House showed its first film.

Courtesy of the Belfast Central Library
Theatre Collection.

In 1897 Daniel Lowrey left the Empire as a result of his misjudgements, with the strains of *For He's a Jolly Good Fellow* still ringing in his ears. He made a brief speech on his last night and the *Belfast Newsletter* reported that he had established himself as a favourite with the public and the artists. He returned to Dublin, where he opened the Empire Palace Theatre on 15 November 1897. Sadly, on 16 August 1898 he died of a brain tumour. Today, the Empire Palace Theatre is known as the Olympia. The Belfast Empire staged one show each evening until this advertisement appeared on Monday 9 May 1904 in the *Belfast Telegraph*:

The Management beg to announce that on and after Monday next, the 16th, the TWO PERFORMANCES A-NIGHT SYSTEM will be adopted.

On Tuesday 17 May its notice was triumphant:

GIANT SUCCESS! EVERYBODY SAYS SO! BOTH HOUSES PACKED!

Meanwhile, back at the Belfast Empire, Con Salmon was steering it out of the doldrums, and by 1902 the theatre was 'making rapid strides towards financial improvement', probably because of Salmon's point-blank refusal to break with its music hall tradition.

31

Right from the off he brought in top music hall stars for his Belfast audience, such as the already mentioned Charlie Chaplin, Marie Lloyd, Eugene Stratton, Harry Lauder, Vesta Victoria and an endless list of others. Later, a youthful Julie Andrews went on stage here with her parents.

Marie Lloyd, whose sister would come to the Empire at the beginning of July 1934 to present 'The Lloyd Family', first came to Ireland in 1891, and toured around. She was reportedly earning £100 a week at that time. Nine years later she appeared on the Empire stage.

Her family name was Wood and in a 1934 advertisement, Daisy Wood was listed along with Marie (Jun), Alice and Rosie. Marie, called Matilda by her family, was born in 1870 and died in 1922, collapsing on stage as the curtain fell. Her private life has been referred to as 'a mess'.

She became known as 'Queen of the Halls', but after her death that mantle passed to Marie Lloyd, who stepped into the limelight with the following song:

The boy I love is up in the gallery, the boy I love is looking at me, there he is. Can't you see? Waving his handkerchief. As merry as a robin that sings on a tree.

Lloyd made her debut aged fifteen. Her first extended tour of the halls in 1892 followed her Irish success, but this was not her first visit. Her best-known songs were, *My Old Man Said Follow the Van, Oh Mr Porter, What Shall I Do?*, and *One of the Ruins That Cromwell Knocked About a Bit.*

The Belfast Evening Telegraph advertised her visit the week before she arrived, starting on Monday 10 September 1900, and she topped the bill from Monday 17 September. The review of Tuesday 18 September read:

The Victoria Square Variety Theatre was crowded last night in every part of the house, the principal attraction being Marie Lloyd, the ever-popular London comedienne, who met with an enthusiastic reception. She was in excellent voice, and it was with the greatest reluctance that the audience allowed her to retire even after a double number of times.

Lily Langtry appeared, Charles Coborn sang his two hits, *The Man That Broke the Bank at Monte Carlo*, and *Two Lovely Black Eyes*, and in a different era the beat policeman slipped in the stage door to sing. Constable Joseph McLaughlin was an instant hit and remained so under his stage name, Joseph Locke.

The big names kept the Empire afloat as the music hall era slipped away, badly hit by the silent movies and the talkies. It created several records during the Second World War, first with its *Come to the Show*, which ran from 1939-1947, celebrating its 150th performance on 28 June 1945, six weeks after V.E. Day. This was followed on 19 June with a Royal Command Performance attended by the Princess Royal. Their Excellencies, the Governor, and the Countess of Granville, were present at the 150th. It was the manager Gerry Morrison's show. In 1939 the Empire wrote itself into the history books when it ignored the warning to close on the outbreak of war. All theatres in the United Kingdom were instructed to do so, and even the famous Windmill Theatre in London obeyed. Gerry Morrison famously rang 10 Downing Street while the war cabinet was in session and spoke to a secretary, pleading his case and arguing that closure was not necessary there.

Eventually, after a long delay, he was given permission to stay open. The scenario can only be imagined—the Prime Minister and colleagues are in an earnest crisis discussion, when the door opens after a timid knock is acknowledged. 'What is it?' snaps the distinctly unamused Prime Minister. 'There's a Gerry Morrison on the phone from Belfast, Prime Minister, he wants to know if the Empire can open tonight.' It must have occurred more or less like that, and shortly afterwards it was confirmed in writing.

The Empire lost just one night and that was because the second air raid in Belfast disrupted the city's electricity supply. Among the local stars to appear was Rinty Monaghan, Belfast's world-champion boxer. Rinty appeared on stage in the week beginning Monday 24 June 1946. Another great champ, Jack Doyle, from the south, performed from Monday 16 April 1945 until the end of the week.

From 1929 until 1939, the Empire players staged performances twice nightly. Stage drama kicked off after the war, and Sam Thompson's controversial *Over the Bridge* opened on 26 January 1960. It was the last hurrah for the theatre and on Saturday 3 June 1961, Bridie Gallagher, Billy Danvers, The Alexander Brothers and Frank Carson brought down the curtain for the last time in front of a packed house.

The Royal Alhambra

The Royal Alhambra Music Hall stood at 41 North Street and while it had its own bar license, it was facing the Deer's Head in Garfield Street, which could also be described as a theatre bar. The Deer's Head is still there today and is well worth a visit. The Alhambra was owned by Dan Lowrey and the site was beside the present-day Northern Ireland Tourist Board Information Centre.

Daniel Lowrey Snr was born in Roscrea in 1823 but, as a young boy, accompanied his parents to England where he grew up. By 1853 he owned a tavern in Liverpool, providing songs and stories for the entertainment of men only. He had built a reputation around the taverns as a singer of comic songs before going out on his own and acquiring several smaller music halls.

Lowrey made his was back to Ireland via Belfast, before ending up in Dublin in a further career move, where he builds on his Belfast experience to create 'The Monster Saloon Music Hall'. The Star was a genuine music hall, charging admission as opposed to a 'free-and-easy', where admission and entertainment were free and money was made from the sale of drink.

Alex Findlater's book *The Story of a Dublin Merchant Family 1774-2001*, gives full details. In 1889 Dan changed the name to 'Dan Lowrey's Palace of Varieties'. Findlater records that 'In July 1890 Dan died at the age of sixty-six' and that 'Daniel the second continued to run the music hall'. When Findlater was looking for someone to run the Empire, young Dan was well qualified for the task.

The first indication that the Alhambra was about to open appeared in the *Belfast Evening Telegraph* of 4 September 1871, stating that Dan Lowrey Snr was the owner and Wat Melton the general manager. One week later, on Monday 11 September, it opened its doors.

It kept them open for eighty-eight years, surviving three major fires before succumbing to the fourth in September 1959. From the opening night, it was typical music hall fare all the way through to that first disastrous fire over the weekend of Saturday 27 February. A complete rebuild was necessary but, in the middle of this activity, Dan Lowrey had a Belfast night in the Ulster Hall on 15 May that was said to have been of a very high quality.

When the Alhambra reopened on 8 September 1873, Dan Lowrey was still the manager, and the improvements of this 1,000-person-plus theatre were the best money could buy. The advertisement advised 'see bills' for details and the starting time was down as '7 1/4'.

Grand opening of the above magnificent palace. A programme of unprecedented
Attractions endless Amusements rendered by a matchless company.

During the next few years Mr Fred Sanders was its manager. Any connection he had with Mrs E. H. Sanders, proprietress of the New Colosseum Hotel, has not been established. In 1879 Lowrey took control of The Star, Dublin. The Alhambra was sold to Mr and Mrs W. J. Ashcroft and it

opened for the new season on Monday 11 August 1879. The appropriate advertisement lists him as sole proprietor and her as director, with John J. Stamford as the general manager (who wrote the evergreen McNamara's Band for his mentor in 1883).

Willie John was an extremely talented Irish-American who also visited the music hall circuit on the British mainland. He featured as 'Muldoon, the Solid Man', and had a turbulent, at times scandalous, private life, which seemed to endear him to Belfast audiences, lived as it was in the public eye. Brawls and punch-ups were commonplace, yet for over thirty years his career flourished. The reason for his appearance in Belfast was simple—he had had enough of his parents, both Ulster-born, and he arrived in Northern Ireland determined to succeed.

Harry Lauder made his professional debut in Belfast and went on to make frequent visits to all the halls in the city, like so many other superstars. He was one of hundreds of high-profile entertainers, backed up by thousands of others in support roles.

Ashcroft combined such entertainment as wrestling (including ladies' events) and boxing, but what kept the venue in the public eye as it continued to be successful was the stream of big names such as Lauder, Dan Leno, Gertie Gitana, Charles Coborn, Florrie Forde, Vesta Tilley, and almost any other you cared to name—the list is endless and also includes Charles Chaplin—

Opposite left: Belfast Telegraph, 17 September 1900

Opposite right: Advertising Marie Lloyd's appearance at the Empire (Mander & Mitchenson, 1965).

Right: 22 July 1901. Courtesy of the Belfast Central Library Theatre Collection.

Charlie's father starring in the week beginning 21 January 1889.

The Alhambra had a number of bars but one big attraction was that it was possible to have a drink while standing at the back to watch the show, and not pay. For twenty years it was at the top and reigned supreme until the opposition caught up.

The first challenger was the Olympia Palace, which opened on the corner of Glengall Street and Glengall Place. Shortly after this the Star in Church Street appeared, followed by the Empire in Victoria Square and the Grand Opera House. They were all well attended and proceeded to nibble away at the Royal Alhambra's address.

The Royal Alhambra dated its Diamond Jubilee from Ashcroft's launch in 1879 and by 1939 it had seen twenty million sit down to watch its shows. Exaggeration? Probably not, for the music hall was the place to be. The Alhambra took its lead from both the Empire and the Star by admitting women to its shows, albeit to boost attendance. Within a month of each other, two stars in the supernova bracket had visited. The second was Paginini Redivivus, the celebrated violinist.

The Royal Alhambra continued with variety until the advent of the movies. It began advertising its Bioscope in 1902, retained its music hall image, kept its liquor license and showed

Rinty Monaghan, Belfast's World Champion Boxer, as advertised in the Belfast Telegraph, 26 June 1946.

Courtesy of the Belfast Central Library Theatre Collection.

Above left: Belfast Telegraph, 16 April 1945.

Above right: The Alhambra Theatre, drawn by T. McNally.

Right: The sheet music for one of Charles Chaplin's hit songs (Mander & Mitchenson, 1965).

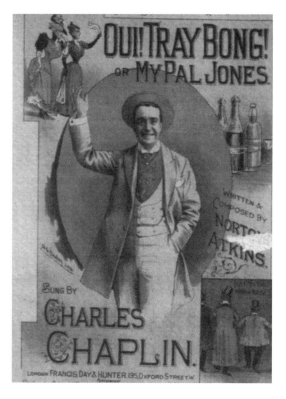

ROYAL ALHAMBRA MUSIC HALL,

41, NORTH STREET, BELFAST.

Sole Proprietor, ... DAN LOWREY.
General Manager, .. Mr. WAT MELTON.

DAN LOWREY most respectfully announces
to the public of Belfast and its vicinity
that, at an enormous expense, he intends Opening
a most magnificent

MUSIC HALL,

at 41, NORTH STREET, on MONDAY, Sept.
11, with a powerful company of

STAR ARTISTES,

And assures those who patronise him with their
presence that the Entertainment will be such as
shall call forth the praise of the most fastidious.

The beautiful Act Drop and costly Decorations
by Mr. J. Keith, of Liverpool; magnificent Gasa-
liers and Sunlights, by Riddel & Co.; Gas-fittings,
&c., by Mr. Stewart.

SPLENDID BAND,

Conducted by an efficient Leader.
Centre Seats, 1s; Side Seats, 9d; Body of
Hall, 6d.   3647

Belfast Evening Telegraph, Monday 4
September 1871.

Left: Belfast Evening Telegraph, Monday 11
September 1871.

Opposite, above left: Belfast Evening Telegraph,
Monday 12 May 1873.

Opposite, above right: Opening night at
the Alhambra, Monday 11 August 1879.
Courtesy of the Belfast Central Library
Theatre Collection.

Opposite below: This advert refers to
Charles Chaplin, father of Charlie
Chaplin. *Belfast Evening News,* from the
week beginning Monday 21 January 1889.

Above left: Courtesy of the Belfast Central Library Theatre Collection.

Above right: W.J. Ashcroft was the star of this Empire show. *Belfast Telegraph*, Monday 21 December 1908.

a mixture of film and variety acts until the Second World War. The man behind the Alhambra's success was declared bankrupt in November 1900, partially due to the decline in audiences and resulting loss of revenue but even after his enforced 'retirement' he continued to travel and perform. This advertisement should be with others in the Empire chapter, but is included here as a tribute.

Ashcroft's health had been failing for a number of years and the *Belfast Telegraph* paid tribute to him on Thursday 3 January 1918, following his death the previous day. The article stated that he was born a showman, beginning his acting career as a child in his father's cellar where he staged regular 'shows'. He went on to become a famed Irish comedian with a remarkable stage career. No doubt the city felt his loss acutely.

As the war approached, the Alhambra suffered two fires in the same year. The first occurred overnight on 13 April, following a cine-variety evening, and the second in February 1940. The

Above left: Belfast Evening News, Wednesday 13 January 1886. Later in 1886, the featured artist, Mr Charles Coborn, reached the top of the charts with his hit song *Two Lovely Black Eyes*, originally called *My Nellie's Blue Eyes*.

Above right: Belfast Evening News, Wednesday 10 February 1886.

Alhambra faced a six-month recovery period after both incidents. Interestingly, the screening on Thursday 13 April featured Ronald Reagan in *Sergeant Murphy*, with the two halls giving comedy support. Two screen idols reopened the cinema on 23 October—Errol Flynn and David Niven performed daring deeds in *Dawn Patrol*.

On both occasions the Royal Alhambra bounced back and pressed on, but on Thursday 10 September 1959, fire took hold of the roof and it eventually collapsed onto the floor below. This time there was no way back. It was a sad ending for a veteran music hall.

The Olympia Palace

By all accounts, Monday 11 May 1891 was a fine day, and as it continued into the evening, it was noticeable that more people than usual were moving down the new Great Victoria Street in the direction of the city centre.

Previously known as the New Dublin Road, it became increasingly crowded upon reaching the Ulster Railway Station, and while some exiting the station probably crossed the street to the Ulster Hotel and Crown Bar, most would have swung left and headed for the nearby corner of Glengall Place.

Glengall Place, a short terrace stretching as far as Grosvenor Road, was occupied by five separate premises. On Grosvenor Road corner, numbers one and two were now a Temperance Hotel. It is interesting to see that when the Royal Hippodrome arrived here, that it was a Temperance Theatre.

No. 3, was occupied by a plumber, and No. 4 by the then-merchant E.J. Freytag. That evening it was the occupant of No. 5 Glengall Street who was responsible for the stir of excitement among the ever-increasing numbers gathering there.

Many were well used to being there, although for a different reason. Tonight it boasted a magnificent new building proclaiming itself to be 'The Olympia Palace—Palace of 1,000 Lights' and its opening-night advertisement clearly signalled its inheritance from the late Ginnett's Circus.

These two advertisements spelt out its closure. It then made way for the Olympia Palace.

The corner site had long been the home of a travelling circus. Harmiston's visited, Cook's came (more of them again) but, at that critical time, Ginnett's were in occupancy. During their stay in 1889, Mr Ginnett was approached by a Methodist clergyman, Dr R. Crawford Johnston, who was seeking the use of his premises for winter services, as the accompanying advertisement shows.

The venue's ability to hold an audience of 2,000 gives an indication of its size and so when Ginnett's decided to move on in the early spring of 1891, a Mr D. Barnard, whose music hall roots lay in southeast England, moved to become the sole lessee and manager, spending freely to improve his new acquisition. He gutted the premises and started from scratch. The advertisement heralding the Olympia Palace's opening, published in the *Belfast Morning News*, spells out the lengths to which he went.

> Mr D. Barnard desires to inform the Gentry and the Public of Belfast that he intends opening the Olympia Palace as a high-class variety theatre, and to provide an entertainment that will surpass anything in the Provinces. Neither time nor money has been spared by him to present an evenings amusement that will repay a visit, even by the most fastidious.

The building was remodelled at a cost of £1,000; the alterations being entrusted to the firm of Messrs Fitzpatrick Bros; the carpets and tapestry to Messrs Robb and Co.; the gas fittings to the older Belfast firm Coats and Co.; and also to Parkes, Belfast, and Houghton and Hodges, London; the grand lounges were furnished by Lyons & Co., theatrical furnishers, London; and a handsome 50 guineas were paid for plush drop curtains, a sprinkling of the best, and all of this was backed up by a 'Full and Competent Orchestra of Sixteen Performers'. He also took care of the health and safety aspects, having firemen in attendance with messengers, livery servants, and page boys.

> Admission – Orchestra Stalls
> (Upholstered and Carpeted) 2s; Pit and Prom – enclave (chairs and carpeted) 1s; Gallery and Second Promenade 6d
> Private Boxes, one guinea, and 10s 6d, single ticket 2s 6d

Having paid and entered that lavish auditorium, and after the orchestra's overture, the lights dimmed and the stars went on to perform what must have been an outstanding show, giving the audience a night to remember.

On her first visit to Belfast was Miss Katie Lawrence ('The Butterfly Queen'), a burlesque artiste from the Empire, London, the Sydney Opera House and Principal Colonial Theatres. Before long, Miss Lawrence would be sending audiences wild with her rendition of 'Daisy, Daisy, give me your answer do'. *Daisy Bell* became a huge hit.

With an enormous salary from the Empire, London, the Elton Troupe appeared in a wonderful gymnastic, acrobatic, eccentric pantomime sketch of a carriage drive and its mishaps.

Other stars on show included operatic vocalists Georgia and Sydney Bell; Mr George Byford, Versatile Comedian; Signorita Eleanora, Queen of the Air—the list went on and on.

The Olympia Palace lasted only a few years and the last advertisement I found appeared on Monday 1 August 1892, although it was there until 1894.

Barnard only stayed for a short time, for on Monday August 1892 there was a 'Grand Reopening—Under New Management'. Mr James Elphinstone became the manager and he, like his predecessors, promoted classic variety theatre, and as far as I could ascertain, he stayed in control until the closure.

AMUSEMENTS.

THEATRE ROYAL
Proprietor and Manager, Mr. J. F. WARDEN
Enormous Success of the Beautiful PANTOMIME
GRAND DAY PERFORMANCE, FRIDAY, Apri
10, at 1-30. Doors open at 1. Early admission
6d extra to all Performances. Roars of Laughter
from Beginning to End. Brilliant Dresses
Superb Scenery. Splendid Music and Ballets
and a most Powerful Company.
THIS (Monday) EVENING, at 7-30,
"CINDERELLA."
GRAND TRANSFORMATION SCENE ANI
COMIC HARLEQUINADE.
FRIDAY EVENING, 10th April, 1891, BENEFIT
of Messrs. WRIGHT and LISBOURNE ("The
Baron" and his Page "Pickles").
Children under twelve Half-price to all parts
except Gallery.   4418

ALHAMBRA THEATRE OF VARIETIES
NORTH STREET.
Proprietor and Manager—Mr. W. J. ASHCROFT.
T. E. Dunville, Eccentric Comedian; Merrie
Rosie, Burlesque Actress and Dancer; Keir and
Allen, Irish Comedians; J. A. Wilson, Negro
Comedian and Dancer; Charlie Murray, Character
Comedian; Sisters De Castro, Duettists and
Dancers; the Lindsays, Musical Comedians; J. P.
Curlett, Irish Comedian and Dancer.
Admission—6d, 1s, and 1s 6d.
Acting Manager—Con. Salmon.   8714

GINNETT'S CIRCUS, GLENGALL
PLACE, BELFAST. FAREWELL PER-
FORMANCES. Last and Best Programme of the
Season. SATURDAY AFTERNOON, April 4th,
1891, Fashionable Day Performance at 2-30. Great
School Treat. All Children, 2d each. SATURDAY
EVENING, April 4th, and during the following
week, the ever-popular Equestrian Spectacle,
TURPIN'S RIDE TO YORK AND DEATH OF
BONNY BLACK BESS. Supported by the whole
of the Company and a host of Auxiliaries.
THIS EVENING, April 6th, 1891, CONUN-
DRUM CONTEST. Prize, £5.
Monday, April 6th; Tuesday, April 7th; Wed-
nesday, April 8th; Thursday, April 9th; Friday,
April 10th; Saturday, April 11th—Last week of
the season—Special and important Engagement of
MINTING, the Marvellous Bicyclist and Spiral
Ascensionist, the Hero of the Wheel. All new
acts in the programme, in addition to Turpin's Ride
to York and Minting.
Wednesday, April 8th, BENEFIT OF VALDO,
the Popular Clown. Extra Attractions.
Friday and Saturday Afternoons, April 10th and
11th, FAREWELL MATINEES and SCHOOL
TREAT. Admission each day for Children, 2d
each. Minting will positively appear at each of
these Performances.
Saturday Evening, April 11th, Last Night, Doors
open at 6-45; commencing at 7-15.
Time and Prices as usual.   7133

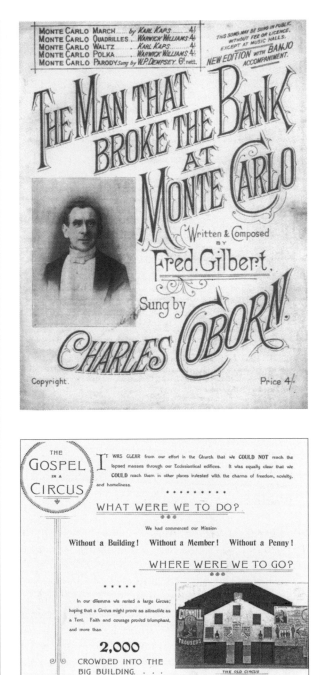

Above left: Ginnett's closure was indicated by this advert in the *Belfast Newsletter*, Monday 6 April 1891.

Above right: Cover of the sheet music (Baker, 2005).

Below right: Ginnett's Circus, courtesy of Belfast Central Mission.

But back now to Friday 24 January 1892, when, in keeping with the custom of the time, the theatre offered a complimentary benefit to its proprietor. All the stops were pulled out for Barnard, and the bill proves, beyond a doubt, the affection in which he was held. It also informs us that the next day there was to be a boxing match.

Barnard's benefit night was a textbook music hall variety show and, in his honour, both the Alhambra and the Bijou Empire did their part by releasing managers. The occasion prompted Willie Ashcroft to send along Con Salmon, while John J. Stamford was given time off from duties at the Bijou. Perhaps he even sang his big hit *McNamara's Band*. Furthermore, artists appearing there were made available for the bill.

It was a splendid occasion with a quality bill played to a full house, although many were left outside in the sharp winter evening, unable to gain entrance. Prior billing had ensured a sell-out for this 'Monster Programme'.

Barnard's complimentary benefit included almost every element that comprised a typical full-bodied variety show: a talented vocalist, a pleasing serio-comic, a new operatic soprano, a comic juggler and equilibrist, American song and dance, Zulima the Iron Queen, the D'Almaine Trio sketch and a troupe of female and male acrobats were among the many acts to entertain that night.

In spite of the restrictions of 'time permitting', John J. Stamford made it onto the stage to sing *The Old Familiar Faces* and the evening was a roaring success.

Mr Barnard moved on, and James Elphinstone promoted the theatre for a short period. A study of the last advertisement I tracked down shows that variety was in good hands. Seemingly nothing happened for several years, although that seems hard to believe. I did a close search for a few months and then at intervals, but it would appear that it lay dormant until it was cleared away to make room for the Grand Opera House.

This was a sad end to what was a splendid building, but at least its replacement would give recognition to the tradition of the 'circus' in its full title. As for Elphinstone and Barnard, they seemed to vanish into thin air.

The Star

On Tuesday 11 October 1892 in Church Street (possibly close to the old theatre that existed there in the 1830s), less than one hundred yards from the Royal Alhambra, a new music hall opened its doors. Its sole proprietor was Edward W. Partrick, previously of the Buffalo Theatre (1882-1889), who, after his short spell at the Star, moved on to become stage manager of the Empire Theatre of Varieties.

Future advertisements also disclosed that Partrick was not only the sole proprietor, but both lessee and manager, and that his premises were at Nos 13, 15 and 17 Church Street. According to the *Belfast Street Directory*, Edward W. Partrick was a 'publican' at this time, for here could be found, not only the theatre, but also the Star Bar as well.

It is thought that they were separated by a narrow lane that passed between Nos 15 and 17. Today near to William Street South, where the Belfast Electoral Office and St Anne's House can be found.

It is more interesting to approach Church Street from Royal Avenue, down Lower North Street. It is the first street on the left and leads directly to Donegal Street and St Anne's Cathedral. Look for the sign with the lettering R.A.O.B. affixed to the wall and suspended overhead. The number 17 is affixed to the plaque. The site of the Star Music Hall is now the headquarters of the Royal Antediluvian Order of Buffaloes-Grand Lodge of Ireland, Club H.Q. and Institute.

OLYMPIA (LATE GINNETT'S CIRCUS),
GLENGALL PLACE, BELFAST.
Manager ...   ...   Mr. JAMES ELPHINSTONE.
GRAND RE-OPENING UNDER NEW
MANAGEMENT.
MONDAY, AUG. 1st, and during the Week.
Engagement of the Great London Novelty
the WALES TROUPE and their Marvellous
Skating Dog "Bogie." Expensive Engage-
ment of TOM BASSETT. Starring Engage-
ment of Mddle. CARR LYON. Special
Engagement of the Demon King of Ventrilo-
quilists, Comical CRIS. Important Engage-
ment of NITA and NIKITA. For six nights
only, the TWO KEAYS (Edith and Arthur).
Miss NORRIE BRANDON; WALTER
OSBORNE and Miss EMMA WATSON;
O'RILEY and CALLAGHAN; Miss DORA
DOUGLAS; BOHEMIAN QUINTETTE of
LADY DANCERS.
For Six Nights Only
FUN ON THE BRISTOL.
TOM LISBOURNE as "Widow O'Brien."
supported by Mr. Ernest Cave, Mr. Will Carson, Mr. W. Sommerfield, Miss Ida Cunardy,
and Mr. A. Thompson. The Grand Ship Scene
direct from the Princess Theatre, Glasgow.
Doors Open at 7. Commence at 7.30. Price
of Admission from 6d to 21s. Half Price to
all parts except Gallery at 9. Early Doors at
6.30 6d extra. Box Office Open at Hall from
10 to 1. Season Tickets £2 2s and £1 1s.
3709

Belfast Morning Post,
Monday 1 August 1892.

OLYMPIA PALACE
Managing Director.....Mr. D. BARNARD.
MONDAY, August 31st, and during the Week,
most expensive engagement of the Season.
£50—FOR ONE WEEK—£50.
SPECIAL NOTICE.
The London Society Comedian,
MR. CHARLES COBURN,
("Two Lovely Black Eyes").
Supported by a First-class Company of Star
Artistes, including the "Tandem,"
Captain Clive's Wonderful Dog, and 7 other
Artistes.
Comic Sketch—"Anna Maria."
Monday next—KENNATTE, Flying Star.11898

Belfast Newsletter,
3 September 1891.

NEW STAR MUSIC HALL

CHURCH STREET.

SOLE PROPRIETOR—E. W. PARTRICK.

OPEN TO-NIGHT

WITH A

FIRST-CLASS VARIETY COMPANY.

Full particulars, see Day Bills.

5027

Left: The opening of the Star Music Hall was advertised in the *Belfast Telegraph* on Tuesday 11 October 1892.

Opposite left: Belfast Telegraph, Wednesday 22 November 1893.

Opposite right: Belfast Telegraph, Wednesday 18 July 1894.

The Star's opening went well and the newspaper advertisement, for its second week, proclaimed 'The Opening an Unequivocal Success' but yet again there is no indication of admission charges. To learn about the then-prices of admission and opening the house, please see the bills.

The owner boasts that he has engaged 'Another Big Company' which included sailor Baylie in his great scene 'Life on the Ocean Wave'. Baylie seemed to be popular in the city for he appeared regularly in various halls. Also performing were The Ashley Skating Trio, The Valleans-Greatest of all Jugglers, Sisters Ely-The Versatile Vocalists, and Caralla and Thomas in the Greatest Rinley Act of All Time. (What exactly is a Rinley act, one wonders.)

While self-praise may be no recommendation, it must be said that Partrick's bills were packed with high quality and wide-ranging variety-time acts. Business must have been good, for before his second season opened on 8 August 1893 he had refurbished his theatre and commenced with another star-studded bill.

It can't have been business failure that prompted Partrick to consider selling out, but rather the lure of a new challenge, and launching the Empire would certainly have been just that. So after two seasons he relinquished control, moved on and handed over the reins to Redmond Jennings, who moved to upgrade the theatre for his opening night.

Before leaving the Star Music Hall, it is worth speculating that perhaps Partrick borrowed the title from the then-defunct Star Saloon in Ann Street, which had wound up as the Alhambra Concert Room, and in time may have suggested to Dan Lowrey the title for his new venture. However, before taking on its new title an advertisement was posted. News that the former Star Music Hall was about to reopen under new management was broken to the public by Redmond Jennings in the *Belfast Evening Telegraph* notice of Wednesday 18 July 1894.

The Star Bar was to be the new music hall's theatre bar, just as the Shakespeare was for the theatre in Arthur Street and the Kitchen Bar (1859) would become for all the various titles in the Empire's patch on Victoria Square.

Although slightly behind schedule, Redmond Jennings fulfilled his promise. However, when he presented his new theatre to the public, not only had it a new name, but he himself had taken a new (stage) name. The opening date was Monday 1 October 1894. The advertisement let all

know that he was no rookie, having been in the business in Norwich.

When Dr Redmond launched his Star Palace of Varieties, he was aware that the Belfast Empire would be stiff competition and he began to charge what he called 'the People's Prices': reserved balcony, 9d; stalls and side seats, 6d; and body of the hall, 4d.

He showed his astuteness on the night that the Empire Theatre of Varieties opened (3 December 1894). Obviously aware that there would be many disappointed theatre-goers in Victoria Square, he put on a bumper show and kept his prices the same.

The bills continued to be of a high standard, but then it simply 'disappeared'. It took me some time to find its last night, Saturday 1 June 1895. On the previous Monday, Dr Redmond announced both its impending closure and his benefit night, arranged for Friday 31 May. The Star then closed for alterations.

It appears to have continued although I found no advertisement until one appeared in the *Evening Telegraph* on Tuesday 5 November 1907 that introduces the Office (previously the Star).

When the last advertisement for the Office is printed on Tuesday 5 May 1908, the owner and licensee are named as James W. Gayle. Street directories show this to be the case from 1904 to 1908.

On 9 September it moved its allegiance to silent movies, before ending its days as a 'Theatre of Varieties' on 27 February 1909.

Left: *Belfast Telegraph*, Tuesday 25 September 1894.

Below: *Belfast Telegraph*, Monday 1 October 1894.

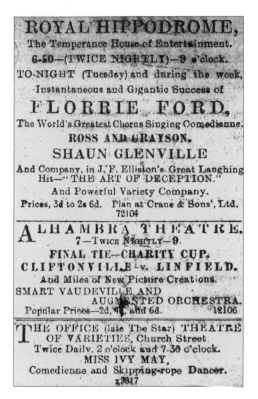

Above left: Belfast Telegraph, 3 December 1894.

Above right: Now called The Office. *Belfast Telegraph,* Tuesday 5 May 1908.

Now a cine-variety theatre. *Belfast Telegraph,* Wednesday 9 September 1908.

The Grand Opera House

The New Grand Opera House opened its doors to the public on Monday 23 December 1895, and in spite of several hiccups along the way it remained open, making it the only music hall still functioning. Its closure during the summer of 2006 enabled improvements backstage, and a new foyer and a smaller theatre facility are to be added. Fittingly, it has spread across the space left when the Royal Hippodrome building was knocked down.

Built on the corner of Glengall Street and Glengall Place, it replaced the Olympia Palace, demolished to facilitate its construction. Its original title was the New Grand Opera House, but from 1900 the 'New' was dropped and, of course, high up on its frontage is an acknowledgement of the circus era: 'The Grand Opera House and Cirque'. It seated 3,500 people, approximately three times today's capacity, and in 1974 it became Belfast's first listed building.

I don't intend to cover every detail of its 112 years. This is already done in Lyn Gallagher's superb *The Grand Opera House, Belfast*, where its full history is given, excluding the more recent developments.

The first permanent hall on the site provided a home for the visiting artists. It was built in November 1882 and became the base for Ginnett's Circus. An idea of its size is given by the fact that at the Gospel Crusade in 1889, 2,000 people crowded into the building.

The Olympia Palace opened in 1891, and its removal in 1894 enabled the opening of the Grand Opera House. Overall, the theatre's interior is little different from 1895, when the main entrance was on the corner. The diagonal advertising space, now visible, was once the front door.

Until recently, the dress-circle bar jutting out above the Great Victoria Street pavement was the most obvious addition. Back in 1895, excellent provision for hospitality on all floors had been made.

Frank Matcham, who designed around 150 other theatres, was among a new breed of architects, and the opera house would not be short-changed. Like elsewhere, there were bars on every floor, serving tea, coffee, food and a wide range of alcoholic beverages, plus cigars and cigarettes.

Digressing a little, it has been very interesting and informative to see many advertisements for the theatres, halls and saloons stressing the fact that separate smoking rooms were available on their premises for the convenience of those who wished to smoke. Very pertinent for this time!

While I have described the interior theatre buildings, I don't intend to do so for the Grand Opera House, which is familiar to many. If you are not familiar with it, go along one evening, or attend one of their open mornings, and see the magnificent décor with its strong Middle Eastern influence. Study the elephants' heads high up at the corner of the gallery. I will shortly be sharing a secret about one of them.

The building of the New Grand Opera House was the result of Joseph Fred Warden's ambition to expand his theatrical influence. He considered the Theatre Royal to be too small, and after the disastrous fire of 1881, it was now up and running. To fulfil his dream, he called in Frank Matcham, the leading theatre architect of the day. The 1890s were the peak years of the music hall era. However, in the early years, the new theatre concentrated on more serious theatre than variety shows.

Warden came from Hull and had just celebrated his fifty-ninth birthday when he launched his new venture. He had been an actor of note, well known across Ireland and the United Kingdom, not only to the theatre-going public but also among his professional peers, which explains the apparent ease with which he attracted leading actors and actresses to Belfast.

I have mentioned elsewhere that Sarah Bernhardt, Mrs Patricia Campbell and Lily Langtry had appeared at his Theatre Royal. Eventually they added the new Opera House to their résumés. They were in good company, for Warden delivered their male counterparts in due course: Martin Harvey in mid-October 1889, and Forbes-Robertson at Halloween 1900, just a

The Grand Opera House, Hippodrome and Ritz Cinema during the Second World War. Courtesy of the Belfast Central Library Theatre Collection.

fortnight after Mrs Langtry. The flow continued, Sir Henry Irving making a return visit to act in the *Merchant of Venice* and *Faust*, commencing Monday 10 November 1902, with his co-star being Ellen Terry. All were leading Shakespearian actors.

The first favour called in by Warden brought yet another notable Shakespearian thespian to Belfast, for what was the official opening of the theatre exactly a week before the curtains rose. Frank Benson, whose company returned every year after the Christmas pantomime, made an appropriate speech. Among those present was Mr G. W. Wolff, of shipyard fame.

The unveiling of a plaque at the launch was attended by the press. The media loved it and lavished praise on the buildings, just as they did at the grand opening on 23 December. A strange irony links the two occasions. Wolff was enjoying a splendid, convivial evening of hospitality and socialising, and then presumably attended the gala opening with the other dignitaries. Imagine how he must have felt on picking up the newspaper to read the *Belfast Telegraph*'s reviewer's comments about the evening, only to see the following boxed announcement just above the review itself:

> Sir Edward Harland Bart., M.P.
> As we go to press it is with deepest regret that a telegram has been received at the Town Hall today, announcing the sudden death last night at Glenfarne, Enniskillen of Sir Edward Harland, Bart., M.P., for North Belfast.

Wolff, almost appropriately, was Member of Parliament for East Belfast, where most of his workforce lived.

New Grand Opera House,
Great Victoria Street, Belfast

Mr Warden requests the pleasure
of your Company at the Unveiling of
Memorial Stone,
by
F. R. Benson, Esq.
and Inspection on Monday 16th Decr at 6.30 p.m.
Mr Stanley Ferguson

An invitation to the unveiling of the memorial stone, to be held on Monday 16 December 1894. Courtesy of the Belfast Central Library Theatre Collection.

Back now to the advertisement placed in the *Belfast Telegraph* on Monday 23 December 1895.

THE NEW GRAND OPERA HOUSE

OPEN TO THE PUBLIC THIS MONDAY EVENING DECEMBER 23RD

One of the most beautiful and substantial structures in the three kingdoms.
Frank Matcham; Architect, London
H. & J. Martin, Belfast, Contractors

The next evening the newspapers carried a full report of the proceedings and described the theatre as 'this truly magnificent place of amusement'. Lord Arthur Hill MP spoke from his box to declare the New Grand Opera House open. Captain McCalmont in the box opposite seconded, and then Joseph Warden came forward making reference to what he had said the previous April on the occasion of his thirty-first benefit at the Theatre Royal in Arthur Square: 'I promised you a theatre second-to-none in the kingdom and one worthy of this great improving city. I ask you now ladies and gentlemen, have I kept my word?'

After his address, in which he described Frank Matcham as 'The King of the Architects', he implored the audience to embrace 'its new friend', but 'don't let us forget our old one in Arthur Square'. Following all this, the architect was called forward for his deserved bow and, the formalities over, the curtain rose on *Blue Beard or Is Marriage a Failure?* It was the first of many pantomimes and was described as being original, funny and blood-thirsty.

There were performances on Christmas Day, Boxing Day and on Friday 27 at 1.30 p.m. When the season ended, the staging of Shakespearian plays began, and this tradition continued for years. Easter pantomimes also became a much-loved tradition.

Forbes Robertson started his week-long run, referred to previously, on Monday 29 October 1900. The audience arriving that evening found that a new entrance to the orchestra and pit stalls had opened, and were directed to the fourth door on the right in Glengall Street. It was stated that 'the entrance to the orchestra stalls by the main entrance will be used only as the dress-circle entrance'.

The improvement meant that patrons had straight passage into the building, whereas before it had been a case of ascending and descending flights of stairs. This alteration came two years after Fred Warden took over as manager, succeeding his father at the turn of the century.

In 1904 a change of direction took place. The Wardens decided that all serious drama should move to the smaller Theatre Royal and that the venue should be renamed 'The Palace Theatre of Varieties'. It became a genuine music hall, operating twice nightly at 7 p.m. and 9 p.m. for the five years between 1904 and 1909.

Its ideal location, a short distance from the Great Northern Railway Station, with its entrance where the Europa Hotel stands, facilitated its audience from the country towns. They would flock to the 7 p.m. show and return home, to Lisburn and beyond, by train, leaving the city folk to enjoy the second house.

The temporary demise of the Grand Opera House followed the final performance of the Christmas pantomime on 16 January 1904. Programme notes and public advertisements heralded the advent of 'The Palace Theatre of Varieties which will open next month'. It did so on Monday 13 February 1904.

It immediately adopted twice-nightly showings at 7 p.m. and 9 p.m. and matinees on Saturdays at 2.30 p.m. The prices ranged from 3d to 1s 6d. It is worth setting out the first variety bill, for subsequently the patterns were the same, with minor variations on the content:

Nelsons Original Newsboys Quintet,
Farrimund – The Lancashire Singing Collier,
The Lorna Trio – World Gymnasts,
The Ferrandre-May Trio – Novelty Entertainers,
Sensational Paper Tearers,
Mdmclle Madji – The Hindoo Marvel, Dancer, Contortionist and Hand Balancer,
Hayes Brothers – Australian Comedy Talkers and Dancers,
Palace Pictures,
Leighton – The Man at the Piano,
Bob Hindec – Comedian,
Tom Vine – Vocalist, Author, Composer,
Clara Nesbitt – Character Vocalist and Burlesque Dancer.

The Palace packed them in for nearly five years before the decision to shut down was made. Audience numbers had begun to dwindle and the impending closure was made known to the public on 23 January 1909, as the annual pantomime *Jack and Jill* finished its run. The notice in the *Ireland Saturday Night* read:

Warden Limited

Notice to the Public

NEW

Grand Opera House
AND CIRQUE.

Great Victoria Street,
Belfast.

Great Victoria Street,
Belfast.

Proprietors, ... "WARDEN, LIMITED." Managing Director, ... Mr. J. F. WARDEN.
Business Manager. ... ... Mr. Fred W. Warden. | Secretary, ... Mr. A. A. Macaulay.

MR. WARDEN begs to announce that the above Magnificent Building will

OPEN TO THE PUBLIC
MONDAY, December 23rd next
ONE OF THE MOST BEAUTIFUL AND SUBSTANTIAL STRUCTURES IN THE THREE KINGDOMS,

FRANK MATCHAM, Architect, London.
H. & J. MARTIN Contractors, Belfast.

Above: The architect who designed the Grand Opera House, Frank Matcham of London, designed over 150 theatres throughout his career. The proprietor, Joseph F. Warden, was a professional actor who performed in the Theatre Royal, among other venues. *Belfast Evening News*, 20 December 1895.

MONDAY, 23rd December, 1895, at 7-30 ; TUESDAY, 24th December, at 7-30 ; WEDNESDAY, 25th December (Christmas Day), at 1-30 ; WEDNESDAY, 25th December (Christmas Night), at 7 ; THURSDAY, 26th December (Boxing Day), at 1-30 ; THURSDAY, 26th December (Boxing Night), at 7-30 ; FRIDAY, 27th December, at 1-30 and 7-30 ; SATURDAY, 28th December, at 7 ; and until further notice.

THE FUNNY PANTOMIME, entitled :—

"BLUE BEARD"
Or, IS MARRIAGE A FAILURE?--The Blue Room and the Tragic Key.
Written Expressly for this Theatre by W. H. RISQUE.

New and Magnificent Scenery, Designed and Painted by Messrs. BRUNTON, TRITCHSLER, BARRY PARKER, and KINNIMONT. **The Music,** Composed, Selected, and Arranged by Mr. J. DALNY BURROWS (Musical Director). **The Charming and Costly Costumes** expressly Designed by Mrs. DOTTRIDGE. The Intricate Scenery, Wonderful Mechanical Effects and Changes by Mr. E. BAX. The Elaborate Properties and Appointments by Messrs. ROBINSON and CAMPBELL. The Limelight, Gas Effects, and Illuminations by Mr. T. E. WARDELL. The Armour by Messrs. KENNEDY & Co., Birmingham. The Comic Scene Invented by Messrs. BERTRAM & RYDON. The New and Popular Songs introduced by kind permission of Messrs. FRANCIS, DAY & HUNTER, ASCHERBERG & Co., HOPWOOD & CREWE, REYNOLDS & Co., DEANE & Co., etc.

The Pantomime produced under Supervision of Mr. ERNEST DOTTRIDGE, and Stage Managed by Mr. F. A. MARSTON
Under the Personal Direction of Mr. CHAS. H. LONGDEN.

Characters by

Miss VERA GRAY.
Mr. LESLIE CLARE.
Mr. FRED A. MARSTON.
Misses WILFORD & WILLS.
Mr. H. J. HOUSDEN.
Mr. STEVE COOKE.
Miss CISSIE MOXON.
Miss FRANCES COVENTRY.
THE SISTERS PARIS.
Mr. GEORGE RYDON.

Misses Polly Desmond, Alice Brown, Jenny Brown, Lottie Gordyn, Mabel Hews, Gladys Debell, Gussie Templeton, Sarah McKay, Flo Andrews, Ella Rosa, Mabel Clarke, Trissy Cornby, Minnie Cornby, Minnie Menzies, Nelly Morris, Alice Peveril, Flora Peveril, Nelly Royale, Edith Jones, Jennie Risley.

Primrose Ballet Troupe.
Ballet Mistress: Madame Eugenie.

SYNOPSIS OF SCENERY.

Scene 1. Anywhere
Scene 2. A Street in Bagdad
Scene 3. Road to Blue Beard's Palace
Scene 4. The Palace Kitchen
Scene 5. An Antechamber
Scene 6. The Palace Gardens
Scene 7. The Courtyard
Scene 8. The Blue Chamber
Scene 9. The Ante Chamber

Scene 10. GRAND TRANSFORMATION, "NIGHT AND MORNING."

Grand Harlequinade

Left: Announcing the opening of the Grand Opera House, 23 December 1895. *Belfast Evening Telegraph.*

Above: Belfast Evening Telegraph, Saturday 27 October 1900.

Below: The Palace Theatre of Varieties. The word 'CIRQUE' appears on the building as this was built on the site of a popular circus. Courtesy of the Belfast Central Library Theatre Collection.

Opposite, below: Courtesy of the Grand Opera House and Blackstaff Press.

BELFAST OPERA HOUSE ON FIRE

EARLY MORN OUTBREAK

GALLERY BADLY DAMAGED

SAWDUST GUARDS CARPET

Unrehearsed drama was provided by a startling outbreak of fire at the Grand Opera House, Belfast, this morning, which resulted serious damage to the gallery and the roof of the theatre.

The Opera House was imperilled by the fire, which was di covered at seven o'clock. The Belfast Fire Brigade made a prom turnout, and their remarkably fine fight resulted in all peril to the theatre being removed.

The gallery suffered worst. The back portion was burnt ou and three rows of seats were charred beyond recognition. The flam forced their way through the ventilators to the roof, which also wa damaged.

There will be no performance at the Opera House to-night, bu herculean efforts are being made to have the theatre ready for reopen ing to-morrow night.

Damage to the theatre itself is estimated to be in the region of from £7,000 to £10,000, but the consequential loss is also heavy.

SAWDUST ON FLOORS

There were many remarkable features connected with the outbreak.

The turntable fire escape was run up 20 feet, and a fireman on the top of it was able to direct effectively the water on the blazing parts. In consequence of the volume, the water trickled down through the various floors to the stalls, where there were minor streams.

The firemen brought in sawdust, which was spread over the floor almost half a foot deep to save the carpet. The water was also trickling down on to the seats, and tarpaulins were procured to cover them. Similar precautions were taken on the dress circle, which was affected in like fashion. There were also small pools in the corridors.

It was a saddening sight to see the havoc of the water in the theatre, which is so attractively furnished.

The safety curtain was dropped, and the stage scenery and effects were not damaged in any way.

Chief-Officer Smith told a "Telegraph" representative that the call was received at seven o'clock and a prompt turnout was made.

"Smoke was issuing from every door and window," he said, "and the theatre seemed doomed.

"The outbreak was located in the gallery where it had a firm hold. A number of lines of hose were brought into action, and after three-quarters of an hour the fire was checked.

"The flames had spread through the ventilators to the roof, part of which was also damaged.

"The turntable fire escape was also in action, and from a height of 70 feet a fireman was able to effectively direct the water on the roof.

"We spread a large number of bags of sawdust over the floors to save the carpets as much as possible, and tarpaulins were also used to cover the seats to prevent the upholstery being damaged."

"HEARTRENDING," SAID MR. McCANN.

Mr. James M'Cann, the "Belfast Telegraph" representative that he received a message early this morning that the theatre was on fire and hurried to the Opera House.

"The gallery has borne the brunt of the fire," he said, "and the stage as well as the remainder of the different parts of the house like the stalls and dress circle has not been affected. It is a heartrending bit but fortunately the run of the show is not likely to be interrupted to any great extent for the "White Horse Inn" has been very popular and the bookings are very heavy for the next fortnight.

"It is a mysterious fire, and I suppose due to a smouldering cigarette end which was carelessly thrown away by a patron in the gallery last night. I left the theatre at 11.30, and everything was then right."

THE FIRST WARNING.

The first warning of the fire was given by Constable Pepper, who rang up the Fire Brigade. Head-Constable Murphy and Sergeant Barry, with a force of police, were speedily on the scene, and gave much appreciated help.

When a "Telegraph" representative visited the theatre soon after the fire he witnessed the extraordinary sight of sawdust being spread all over the floors.

"We are trying to save your carpet," said Chief Officer Smith to Mr. M'Cann who ruefully watched the firemen at work Scores of tarpaulins covered the seats, and this precaution was a wise one.

It was a melancholy sight to see the pools of water forming in the corridors. Hose were not immune from its ravages.

Water streamed down the corridor leading to the gallery, and the scene in this portion of the house was well nigh incredible.

Half a dozen firemen were trying to subdue a troublesome spot in the centre of the gallery, from which small spurts of flame appeared.

Chief Officer Smith, whose sole desire was to minimise the damage from the water advised the men to try a handpump, and soon gave a full blast. Anxiety for the safety of the building was the keynote of the firemen, who are to be congratulated on their excellent work.

A FEW FROCKS DAMAGED.

Mr. William Youngman, the manager of the "White Horse Inn" Company, told a "Telegraph" representative that the fire had come as a bombshell to all concerned. "It is rarely," he said, "that a occurrence of the kind takes place, and it is all the more unfortunate in the present instance in view of the success of the show in Belfast."

Mr. Harry Warde, the stage manager said that it was fortunate the stage was not involved. "Water has damaged a few of the frocks," he added, "but the lavish scenery of the show has come out unscathed."

GRAND OPERA HOUSE

THIS MONDAY, September 18, 1933.

6-40 —— TWICE NIGHTLY —— 8-50

PERSONAL APPEARANCE OF THE
QUEEN OF VAUDEVILLE,

GRACIE FIELDS

SUPPORTD BY

| THOM & MACK, Acrobatic Comedians. | JACK DALY, Irish Entertainer. |

| CHARLIE HIGGINS 100 per cent. Looney, with BERT BRAY. | Freddie, Phyllis and Anne, Latest Rhythm. |

| TOMMY NINO FIELDS & ROSSINI A Kouple of Komiks. | 3 RASCALS, In Old and New Successes. |

BALLIOL & MERTON.
SENSATIONAL DANCERS.

POPULAR PRICES—6d to 3s. Booking Office daily, 10 to 10. 'Phone 1142.

NEXT WEEK, TWICE NIGHTLY,
CHAPMAN'S GREAT CONTINENTAL

ZOO AND CIRCUS.

EMPIRE. TO-NIGHT at 6-40 and 8-50

JIMMY LAW AND HIS FAMOUS SUPREMES.
PRINCE YOGA, Wonderful Indian Mystic.
SAM RAYNE, "The Irish Playboy."
MARIE LAWTON AND HER HARP.

REVUE. Two Shows in One. VARIETY.
6d—2s 4d. Booking 11 till 8-30. Phone 3155.

Far left: Belfast Telegraph, Wednesday 4 April 1934.

Left: Gracie Fields appeared at the Grand Opera House many times and took over from Marie Lloyd as 'Queen of the Halls'. Belfast Telegraph, 18 September 1933.

The Palace Theatre will be closed for one week to allow for renovations when it will re-open on February 1st with The Gorgeous … play 'Butterflies' and will henceforth be carried on as a First-Class Theatre under the original title The Grand Opera House.

For the next decade, in spite of the horrors of the First World War, it was business as usual but, like other theatres, its smooth running was affected by 'the Troubles' of 1920. The Grand Opera House advertisement of 5 October 1920 was typical of others:

NOTICE

In consequence of the curfew order, the performance at the theatre will commence tonight and until further notice at 6.30.

The details of the production *The Cinderella Man*, featuring Alfred Butt, were also given.

However, the next year another theatre fire came Belfast's way and nearly destroyed the Grand Opera House. Like other cities across the water, Belfast was falling foul of the carelessly discarded cigarette, or the cigar not stubbed out. On the night of 3 or 4 April 1934, a fire broke out in the gallery. Prompt action by the fire brigade saved the day. There was no performance on Wednesday 4, but they resumed on Thursday 5.

The theatre struggled along for a time. Will Fyffe visited in the second week of May but closure was inevitable, for the gallery was structurally unsound. Over the summer, work was carried out, and it opened in August.

During its time as 'The Palace', occasional visits by touring companies took place, and after reverting to its former name these became a regular feature, with shows and music hall coexisting on the stage.

Between the World Wars, Belfast audiences were treated to all the great musicals and were entertained by artists of calibre, such as Will Fyffe and Gracie Fields, who opened the Ritz Cinema (Jury's Hotel is on the site) in the mid-1930s. On her first performance at the London Palladium, Gracie Fields earned a £100 fee, and in 1933 she received a tumultuous welcome. She then continued on to America aboard the *Queen Mary*, accompanied by her pianist Harry Parr Davies. At one stage during the trip, Davies took a stroll on deck and leaned over the rail to look at the waves. To his horror, his spectacles slipped off and fell overboard, leaving him almost blind. In despair, Gracie ran to the purser's office to see if any shops on board sold spectacles, but had no luck. At that moment, a steward appeared and pinned up a notice saying 'Found—a pair of spectacles, apply to the purser'. Davies tried them on, hoping they would be suitable. It turned out they were as good as his own … in fact, they were his own. A passenger in a lower-deck cabin had put his hand out of the porthole to check for rain, and Davies' glasses had fallen right into it.

There have been many other celebrity visits but the undoubted highlight was the appearance of Stan Laurel and Oliver Hardy in April 1952, and still the big names and big shows continue to come as the old theatre blossoms once again.

To do so, however, it had to survive several difficult times. In the late 1970s it had fallen into a poor state and its fate looked all but sealed. However, a state grant that seemed certain to be heading for the Coliseum, on the nearby corner of Sandy Row and Grosvenor Road, was given to the Palace at the last moment.

Then in 1991 and 1993, two huge explosions caused extensive damage, but the building refused to fall and it is now in excellent health and is ever more welcoming.

I have skipped over much of the detail of its life but I recommend readers go to Lyn Gallagher's book for more information. It's nice to have an exclusive with which to end—a real piece of inside information!

My father-in-law, Harry Herdman, an ardent theatre-goer and frequenter of the music hall, was at the Opera House one Saturday night, specifically the second house, up there in the Gods, close to the elephant's head on the left.

Music hall audiences were unforgiving if they considered a performance to be of poor quality, and it was no different in the Gods that Saturday evening, when expectations were not met by a very well-known lady singer and comedian.

She came on stage very definitely and obviously below par and the worse for wear! Perhaps it is good that I genuinely do not recall her name, for to her embarrassment and discomfort a hail of shipyard washers rained down on her and anybody in between if they fell short.

Among them flew a much larger missile—for one patron was so incensed by the performer's offering that he climbed up to the elephant and snapped off its tusk before descending and going to the rail to hurl it in the direction of the stage.

So next time you visit the newly appointed premises, spare a moment to look up at the elephant to your left. Better still, go up and have a look for the crack that shows where it was glued back together.

One last note about the second show on a Saturday. It started a little earlier, and the Liverpool boat was in use to enable the performers to return to the UK for their next show the following week.

Finally, there are two advertisements to look at, both for megastars from Scotland. Harry Lauder was the first music hall star to be knighted (1919), and was a singer of tuneful, lyrical songs. His act was always well prepared. He was born in 1879 and died in 1950. Eventually, he became the highest-paid music hall star, taking over from Gracie Fields, who was made a Dame in 1979.

It is a strange pairing, for Will Fyffe (1855-1944), a first-rate actor, turned to the halls after sketches he had submitted to Lauder were rejected. Confident in his material, he became his own man and is famous for *I Belong to Glasgow*.

The Royal Hippodrome

Although the Royal Hippodrome was in existence for almost ninety years (1907-1996), its music hall days, or variety days, were shorter. In its other life it was the Odeon Cinema (1961) and subsequently the New Vic (1974). It became a cinema for the first time in 1931, when the curtain fell on its variety days, although there were still occasions when world-renowned performers would take to its stage.

The Hippodrome opened on Easter Monday, 1 April 1907, and closed its doors as a music hall variety theatre on Saturday 6 June 1931. It has been claimed, and recorded, that twenty million patrons took their seats throughout those years.

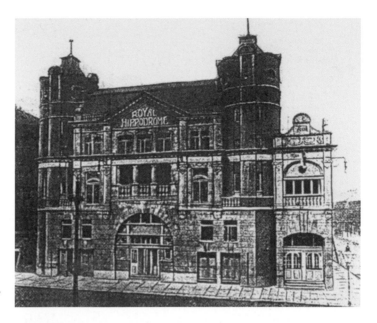

Opposite left: Belfast Telegraph,
8 May 1934.

Opposite right: Belfast Telegraph,
26 February 1934.

Above right: The Royal
Hippodrome. *Belfast Evening
Telegraph,* Saturday 6 April
1907.

Right: Interior view of the
Hippodrome. *Belfast Evening
Telegraph,* Saturday 6 April
1907.

As the photograph shows, the Royal Hippodrome was a large structure with its main entrances to the stalls and circle through doors facing onto Great Victoria Street. Smaller doors led to the gallery up a flight of stairs from both Great Victoria Street and the side entrance in Grosvenor Road, at what had been number one and two Glengall Place and the Ulster Hotel.

It was the last big theatre built in the city and came late to the music hall scene, whose heyday was during the 1890s. It looked better inside, held 2,200 patrons and was very similar in design to its neighbour, the Grand Opera House. It was luxurious and well appointed, having a vast, curved, steeply tiered circle, and balconies with private boxes.

That audience statistic of twenty million seems staggering. However, it is important to remember that Belfast's citizens were great theatre-goers. Seemingly it held performances twice nightly, with a matinee too. Anyone who cares to work it out might have been concerned about low attendance figures!

EMPIRE
7—TWICE NIGHTLY—9.
TO-NIGHT (Saturday),
LAST NIGHT OF
MDLLE. CLASEN'S
LIVING
ART BRONZES
BROXBOROUGH & WRIGHT, in a Farcical
Episode, entitled,
COCKIE.
AND POWERFUL COMPANY.
Prices—3d to 1s 6d.

ROYAL HIPPODROME.
GREAT VICTORIA STREET, BELFAST
Proprietors—Belfast Hippodrome Company
Limited. Resident Manager, Mr. H. T. Down
6-50.—TWICE NIGHTLY.—9.
GRAND OPENING, Easter Monday, 1
April, 1907; and during the Week,
LYDIA YEAMANS-TITUS,
Baby Impersonator,
assisted by Mr. F. J. Titus, Accompanist
MALYELLONI TROUPE, Lady Acrobats,
O'MALLEY & BROWNE. M'CANN'S IRISH
TERRIERS.
WEBB and EDNA BRANSTON.
LESSLIE BROS., Eccentric Musical Comedians
ELLLIN, Ventriloquist. HIPPOSCOPE PICTURES
TSENTANOVIS SISTER
MAGIC ALBUM OF PICTURE POSTCARDS.
HORACE WHEATLEY.
The favourite Comedian and Dancer.
Grand Orchestra. Conductor, Mr. Haines
MATINEES.
Special Matinees, Easter Tuesday and Wed
nesday, doors open at 2, commence 2-30. Full
Programme same as Evening. Prices—Gallery
4 1 Pit, 6d; Circle, 1s; Stalls, 1s 6d; Boxes
5s and 10s 6d, or 2s 6d Single Seat. Booking
at Crane & Sons, Limited, Wellington Place
at House, Doors Open 6-20, commence 6-50;
Second House, Doors Open 8-40, commence
9 o'clock. The Management reserve the right to
refuse admission.

ALHAMBRA THEATRE
TWICE NIGHTLY—7 and 9.
THE ALHAMBRA DRAMATIC COMPANY
Will Present
"THE COLLEEN BAWN,"
Latest Pictures on the Alhambra Bioscope,
THE HOOLIGANS OF THE FAR WEST.
Prices of Admission—3d to 1s.

MADAME CLARA BUTT.
MR. KENNERLEY RUMFORD.
SUPPORTED BY BRILLIANT PARTY,
including Mons. HOLLMAN.
Their last appearance for two years.
ULSTER HALL, Thursday, 11th April, at 8.
Prices, 5/- to 1/-. Tickets at Music Shops.
AED9455

An advert placed on 30/31 March 1907 in the *Belfast Evening Telegraph* for opening night on Easter Tuesday, 1 April.

The media was generous in its praise of the new building. The *Belfast Newsletter* stated, 'It is the handsomest place of entertainment in Ireland'. It must be remembered that when it opened the silent movies were about to be launched, and within three years the Hippodrome would have to fight for its audience, as numerous cinemas had opened.

The ceiling was hand-painted in a delicate design of roses and flowers set off by simple wall decorations, with comfortable seating placed on velvety carpets. The scenery is recorded as being bright and pleasing, with the overall effect described as 'never garish'. One reviewer called it 'a novel feature so far as local places of amusement are concerned'.

Right from day one the Hippodrome was prepared for the Silent Era. The latest cinematographic equipment was in place, and it had fireproof walls, complete with asbestos and emergency shutters. When the time came, the audience was able to watch films alongside variety acts, in the manner of a cine-theatre.

From high above, 'the lantern—a magnificent one—threw a strong steady light, and it was secure and safe, locked inside the projection room, as were the unpleasant fumes'.

Even on its grand opening night it rose to the challenge it faced by introducing Hipposcope Pictures. The proprietors, the Belfast Hippodrome Company, did what the famous Northern

Ireland footballer Danny Blanchflower had advocated, and equalised before the opposition scored. It was to stand them in good stead.

The lack of a big name upon opening was soon forgotten, as one after another they came, just as they did to the other venues. Three weeks after the Hippodrome launch, Eugene Stratton appeared. Like many, he began in a minstrel troupe before migrating to the halls in 1892. American by birth, he soon established himself as a favourite. His top hits were *Little Dolly Daydream* and, the one he was expected to include every time, *The Lily of Laguna*.

He stood on the stage, lit by a single spotlight, and started softly in a pitch that grew in intensity. He was born in 1861 and, like many of the other familiar names, was a member of the 'golden period' that lasted from 1850 until 1880.

From far-away Sydney, via the London stage, came Florrie Forde, arriving in the first week of May 1908. She was already well received in the city. Born in 1876, at the age of seventeen she was an instant hit at home when in her very first performance she sang 'He kissed me when he left me, and told me I had to be brave'.

Forde was a singer of 'big' songs such as *Pack Up Your Troubles, Tipperary, Has Anybody Here Seen Kelly*, or *Hold Your Hand Out You Naughty Boy*. She patrolled the stage, sang with a lusty voice, and entertained the troops during the First World War. Among other songs, she often sang *Goodbye-ee*.

She was preparing to do the same all over again in the Second World War when she collapsed and died in April 1940. She was best known for her rendition of *Down at the Old Bull and Bush*, which was her favourite, and was also adopted as the music hall's signature tune, and even its anthem.

The stars were practically lining up to appear. Two months before Florrie Forde took the stage on Monday 2 March 1908, George Robey starred as 'England's Greatest Comedian, Vesta Victoria-Queen of Eccentric Comedy'. She sang *Daddy Wouldn't Buy Me a Bow Wow* every night from 30 July 1911; Wee Georgie Wood starred at Halloween in 1911 and the Fred Karno's Troupe in early May of that year.

The visit of the great escapologist Harry Houdini arguably takes pride of place. The world-renowned 'Handcuff King' arrived for a week on Monday 25 January 1909, with all seats taken at all performances. His playbills announced 'Houdini accepts Queen's Island challenge' and the highlight of the evening was his escape from an 'airtight, galvanised iron can', filled with water and secured with six padlocks.

All was going well until disaster struck early on Sunday 3 May 1914, when a serious fire ravished the building, and another theatre was devastated by a carelessly discarded cigarette backstage in a dressing room. The nightwatchman had missed it on his inspection round. Most of the damage was backstage, but closure was inevitable.

The timing of the fire was fortuitous, if that is an appropriate way of putting it, for the Grand Opera House was closing for the season and could house the Hippodrome temporarily, until this advertisement appeared (see page 63).

When the theatre was restored to good health, the management played a trump card by bringing over a number of big names, such as Gertie Gitana, 'The Star that Never Fails to Shine', W.C. Fields and Harry Tate. Their biggest name, however, was one that would always pull in the crowds—Bransby Williams.

Williams was born in 1870 and lived until he was ninety-one. He was a seasoned performer who moved with ease between the legitimate stage and music hall. He was a classical actor, in particular a Dickensian one. He was a great character actor; he performed his best-known role, Scrooge, on television. Monologues were his speciality and he introduced many to his audiences, such as *The Green Eye of the Little Yellow God*. His recording of it is superb.

A note appeared on several advertisements and was a reflection of the times in 1920. Below all

Above left: *Belfast Evening Telegraph*, Tuesday 5 May 1908.

Above right: Florrie Forde (Mander & Mitchenson, 1965).

theatre names was written 'During Curfew-One House'. The latest starting time was 7.45 p.m. If there were two houses, then curtain-up was at 5.45 p.m. and 7.45 p.m.

On 13 May 1931, just four weeks before the Hippodrome's music hall days came to an end, the great American Vaudeville artiste, Sophie Tucker, made her first and only appearance in Ireland. She was the last one of the star names of that golden era to visit. Soon the baton would be passed to performer Gracie Fields.

Known for her double entendre, Sophie Tucker made the big time in Chicago in 1910 with *But He Only Stayed Till Sunday* and *I Just Couldn't Make My Feelings Behave*. Famously, she is said to have had a run-in with Hitler in Vienna.

Sophie was born on 13 January 1884 on the Russian-Polish border, as her mother had fled to America to join her father, who was escaping military service. She worked in the family restaurant and earned money by literally singing for her supper.

Her singing of *My Yiddisha Mama* offended the Nazis, and Hitler banned her from singing in Viennese halls, so the crowds amassed as she sang it in the street. She was, like the song she sang, the *Last of the Red Hot Mamas*.

On 29 May 1931 an advertisement announced the closure of the Hippodrome, scheduled for 6 June of the same year.

As on the opening night, there were no front-line performers. What catches the eye is 'D'Alba-Television Wonder Girl'. The question is, how many would have seen her, or even known what television was? The following weekend there was a benefit function for the staff.

Right: Belfast Evening Telegraph, Thursday 7 May (year unknown).

Far right: Belfast Evening Telegraph, Wednesday 29 July 1914.

Six weeks later it had become a 'talkie cinema' and the crowds queued in the street to see the first showings on the big screen of *Resurrection* and *Red Sister*.

Some of its old music hall glory was recaptured following a brave decision by the then-manager, David Forrester, to attract some of the variety shows that were touring Britain. In 1942 a resident band was formed to play at mixed cine and variety performances.

Soon the tradition of a Christmas circus started. It contained the 'full works'—clowns, acrobats, performing dogs, horses and ponies, lions and chimps, novelty acts and jugglers, with trapeze artists swinging to and fro high up in the roof.

I remember being seated at the upper end of the tightrope walker's wire, way up in the Gods. The performer climbed slowly up with the odd manufactured wobble and an occasional slip backwards, his balancing pole swaying dangerously. On reaching the top he slid all the way down. It was all the more breathtaking because there was no safety net.

A footnote to the disastrous fire of Sunday 14 May 1914—a boy named Harry joined the crowd across the road from the Hippodrome that morning. Three other members of his family may have been with him but he never said. Boys being boys, it's likely they were.

In 1916 they were with him at the Somme during the First World War. Harry was enlisted into

Left: Belfast Evening Telegraph, 23 July 1917.

Below: Bransby Williams (Mander & Mitchenson, 1965).

Right: This advertisement in the *Belfast Telegraph* announced the Hippodrome's closure, 1 June 1931.

Below: Sophie Tucker (b.13 January 1884, d.9 February 1966) was billed as 'The Last of the Red Hot Mamas' on British stage. On a visit to Vienna in 1928 she was said to have given an impromptu street performance at the request of a crowd of admirers. *Belfast Evening Telegraph.*

the RIR aged fifteen, and brothers Billy, Jack and Tommy joined as well. All four returned.

My father-in-law Harry Herdman returned, thanks to the silver cigarette case he carried in his left tunic pocket. When the German bullet found its mark, it deflected off the case. He never smoked again funnily enough. What is important is that he, like so many Belfast people, embraced the music hall. Harry had a great tenor voice, sang all the great songs of those days, and on his ninetieth birthday he was heard singing strongly as he walked along the City Hospital corridors. Fittingly, he was singing Harry Champion's hit, *I'm Henry the Eighth I Am, I Am.*

The Alexandra

The Alexandra Theatre was built on the corner of Grosvenor Road and Sandy Road. In time it would become the Palladium and a further name-change to the Coliseum turned it into a cine-variety theatre.

I had read that the Alexandra began its theatre life in 1909 and I therefore spent several fruitless hours keeping an eye out for the name. Having found it, I worked back until I unearthed its first advertisement, at least the first in the *Belfast Evening News*, placed on Wednesday 12 April 1911. There were none before this, but somehow I feel that it may have opened on the Monday or Tuesday.

The Alexandra's opening was eagerly awaited and the building just about matched its near neighbour, the Royal Hippodrome, for size. It was said to be luxurious and kept faith with the interior style of theatres built in the 1890s. It was well carpeted and had several bars and marvellous decorations on the ceiling, with lavish wall carvings. It was new, fresh, and the place to be, and it added its weight to the Belfast theatre scene.

It operated twice nightly and used various epithets to describe itself, never running for long with any particular one. These are best illustrated by looking at several sample advertisements.

However it was primarily theatre rather than variety on the stage, and, even in its earliest days, it struggled to be popular. Therefore it changed its name to the Palladium and maintained the twice-nightly timetable. The grand opening of the Palladium was scheduled for a Monday in late September 1913.

While it was the Alexandra, it tended to stage plays with separate acts as part of an overall programme—for example, Cartney and Sharpe, Ragtime and Alice Ferndale, Belfast's favourite vocalist. A powerful programme was a typical catch-all. Prices varied slightly across its lifetime but remained in the range of 3*d* to 1 shilling.

Situated as it was, just across the Boyne Bridge at Sandy Row, it was a natural habitat for the children of that area, once it had passed its Palladium days and become the Coliseum Cinema. For a time it existed as a cine-variety theatre. It was a puzzle to audience members why the boxes were there.

A further twist in the Alexandra's tale nearly made it the city's opera house. In 1956 plans were in hand to purchase the premises and restore the glory of the inaugural Alexandra. Funding was available but the end product failed to materialise and so the stylish building missed out on restoration and the chance of preservation. Today the site is vacant, hidden behind advertising hoardings, following the Coliseum's closure in June 1959. Its seating capacity was 900.

The *Belfast Telegraph* advertisement of 9 March 1915 proves the authenticity of the Coliseum's claim to cine-variety status:

Right The Alexandra Theatre and Music Hall, sometimes the 'Palladium', found at the corner of Sandy Row and Grosvenor Road. Courtesy of Mr T. Thompson.

Far right: This notice advertises films being shown at the Alhambra over the Christmas period, 1925.

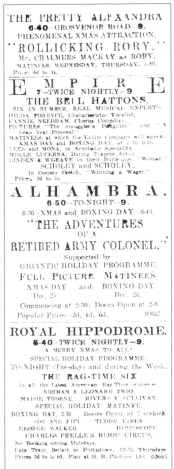

THE PRETTY ALEXANDRA
6-40 GROSVENOR ROAD 9.
PHENOMENAL XMAS ATTRACTION,
"ROLLICKING RORY."
Mr. CHALMERS MACKAY as RORY.
MATINEES, WEDNESDAY, THURSDAY, 2-30.
Prices 4d to 1s.

E M P I R E
7—TWICE NIGHTLY—9
THE BELL HATTONS,
SIX IN NUMBER, REAL MUSICAL EXPERTS.
HILDA FORDYCE, Characteristic Vocalist.
FANNIE NEEDHAM, Chorus Comedian.
PICTURES "The Smuggler's Daughter" and "A Leap Year Proposal."
MATINEES, at which the Entire Company will appear.
XMAS DAY and BOXING DAY, at 2 30 p.m.
LEES and MONA, in Acrobatic Speciality.
MDLLE LUCERNA, Daring Trapeze Artist.
LINDEN & M'GRAVE in their Burlesque, "Woman."
SCHOLEY and SCHOLEY,
In Comedy Sketch, "Winning a Wager."
Prices, 3d to 1s.

A L H A M B R A.
6-50—TO-NIGHT—9.
6-30—XMAS and BOXING DAY—8-45.
"THE ADVENTURES
OF A
RETIRED ARMY COLONEL,"
Supported by
GIGANTIC HOLIDAY PROGRAMME.
FULL PICTURE MATINEES
XMAS DAY and BOXING DAY
Dec. 25 Dec. 26.
Commencing at 2-30; Doors Open at 2-0
Popular Prices —2d, 4d, 6d. 03667

ROYAL HIPPODROME.
6-40—TWICE NIGHTLY—9.
A MERRY XMAS TO ALL!
SPECIAL HOLIDAY PROGRAMME.
TO-NIGHT (Tuesday) and during the Week.
THE RAG-TIME SIX
in all the Latest American Rag-Time Scenes.
NORMAN & LEONARD TRIO.
MAISIE THORNE. RIVERS & SULLIVAN.
SPECIAL HOLIDAY MATINEE.
BOXING DAY, 2.30. Doors Open at 2 o'clock
SISI AND FIFI TEDDY EIREN
GEORGE WALKER HIPPISCOPE.
CHARLES PRELLE'S BIJOU CIRCUS.
No Booking during Holidays.
Late Train, Belfast to Portadown, 10-55 Thursday.
Prices 3d to 1s 6d. Plan at H. R. Phillips, Ltd. 03665

COLISEUM
Grosvenor Road Belfast

A Highway Man's Honour
In three parts. Exclusive to the Coliseum

SIGNOR NERO
Celebrated Italian Instrumentalist
FRED KNOWLES – Burlesque Comedian
6.30 and 9.30 p.m. Admission 2d, 4d, 6d, 1s.
Children half-price to matinees – Mondays 3.30
Saturday at 3.

The Gaiety

At the top of what is today regarded as Upper North Street, stand the remnants of the Gaiety. It stands at the junction with Carrick Hill, under the guise of the Star Bingo Hall.

The Gaiety was purpose-built to be a cine-variety theatre. The theatre made a late entrance into the marketplace and its location at 157-163 North Street was strategic, enabling it to draw its audiences from both the Shankill and Falls Roads. It is said that their residents, by arrangement, shared out the evenings on which to attend.

It had a close link with the Imperial in Cornmarket and an orchestra that drew on the strengths of that cinema's musicians and experience, and, from the opening night, top-rated films were shown and accompanied by this orchestra.

The cine-variety theatre prospered for some years, and the Gaiety benefited from this era, but with the introduction of the talkies, they soon faded into obscurity. Although it had a promising start, the Gaiety, like others, went downhill. The standard of the acts dropped, and while the establishments tried to cling to the image of music hall and retain their earlier successes, eventually reality had to be faced.

When the Alhambra changed course it was more successful in retaining its music hall image, though by 1909 it was showing films twice nightly. It had become the first genuine movie house by 1907.

The Gaiety, in spite of its interior splendour, never quite lived up to its initial promise. The people failed to keep the cashiers busy and it slowly slipped away, closing in 1956.

May Street Music Hall

Once I began winkling out those names that appeared regularly in the amusement columns, I was soon confronted with the apparent problem of May Street Music Hall and Victoria Hall. They appeared to me, as to many others, to have been one and the same. This was also the case for Marcus Patton, who, in his book *Central Belfast*, describes it as the Victoria Music Hall, while Cathal O'Byrne in *As I Roved Out* acknowledged it as the May Street Music Hall, and then the Victoria Memorial Hall, so-called after Queen Victoria.

In 1916 the Brethern Assembly adopted it as their church. It then became Victoria Hall, thus confusing the matter even further. For a time I was lost in a fog, but it cleared when I discovered that all references to the Victoria Hall in its advertisements were headed 'Victoria Street'. The obvious decider that they were, in fact, two different places, came when advertisements for both were placed on the same day, on 8 April 1871:

> On offer to the public – Mons D'Arc's unrivalled Waxwork Exhibition. Cosmoramic Views and Marionette Entertainment. Ten o'clock in the morning till ten o'clock at night.

Immediately below sits the Victoria Hall notice, confirming two different halls at two different locations.

> Poole and Young's New Entertainment – this day at 3 and 8.

The May Street Music Hall opened on the evening of Thursday 26 March 1840, with a grand concert. The doors were to be opened at 7.30 p.m. and the music was to commence at 8.30 p.m. precisely.

Opening Announcement
THE GAIETY
Picture and Variety Theatre

UPPER NORTH STREET,

Will be Open to the Public on and after

TUESDAY, NOVEMBER 14.

(Under the same management as the "IMPERIAL," Corn Market).

The GAIETY is without doubt the most luxurious Theatre of its kind in Ireland.

Performances Twice Nightly—6-40 and 9 p.m.

Popular Prices—**Pit, 2½d. Stalls, 5d. Balcony, 7d** (Including Tax)

Belfast Evening Telegraph, Monday 13 November 1916.

"THE GAIETY"
UPPER NORTH STREET

SHOWING TO-NIGHT—

"The Eternal Grind"

and the different roads they went.

A Famous Players Masterpiece, in Five Acts, featuring the Supreme Screen Star, MARY PICKFORD. A very human story of three sisters in a sweater's factory. A Pickford Classic. Grave, and Gay.

Supported by

LIL CADBURY
The Chocolate Coloured Girl and a Pianist, presenting a Drawing-room Musical, Vocal and Dancing Act. The essence of Refinement and Originality.

PONY SAM
The Celebrated Cowboy Actor Vocalist.

THE GREAT TRANS-ATLANTIC SERIAL PHOTO PLAY—

"PEG O' THE RING" First Episode, Two Parts— "The Leopard's Mark"

This Exploit is comprised of the most thrilling sensations, and Pictures of Comedy, Interest, and Current Events.

Popular Prices of Admission—**Pit, 2½d. Stalls, 5d. Balcony, 7d** Including Entertainment Tax.

Belfast Evening Telegraph, Tuesday 14 November 1916.

The youthful Catherine Hayes from Limerick launched the night at the mere age of fifteen. Miss Hayes earned her first fee of 10 guineas (£10.50) and went on to become a world-renowned prima donna of the concert hall and stage. Nine years later she received £1,400 for the Covent Garden Season.

The music hall was built as a result of the efforts of the ever-expanding Belfast Anacreontic Society, formed in 1814. This amateur music group met to promote both vocal and instrumental music. At first, it met in the Assembly Rooms Commercial Buildings—nowadays the northern-wing building at the Waring Street/Bridge Street corner—and later in the Belfast Savings Bank premises in King Street.

Its popularity, both in membership numbers and concert attendance, forced the society to relocate. The decision to erect the music hall was reached in May 1838, when plans were submitted. 'The building is to hold audiences of up to 600' (Ulster Architectural Heritage Society), while Cathal O'Byrne estimated it could hold 'about 800 persons'. It matters little which is correct. It was said to have a gallery over the entrance and a full orchestral stage in the hall.

An advertisement in the *Belfast Newsletter* on the morning of Friday 28 February 1840 is the first indication that all has gone well in the planning of the venture.

Meeting This Day

NEW MUSIC HALL

A general meeting of the members of the Anacreontic Society, and shareholders in the NEW MUSIC HALL, will be held in the building on Tuesday, the 3rd March, at three pm for the purpose of receiving a Report and Statement of Accounts, from the Building Committee; of determining on public; and transacting such other business as may be brought before the meeting.

John Cameron, Secretary
By Order Belfast 28th Feb, 1840

What satisfaction it must have given Mr Cameron and his committee to sit down in the new hall and set its opening date for the public. He could not have known that by around 1872, its best days would be behind it, due in no small measure to the ever-increasing popularity of the newly erected Ulster Hall (1862), nor that his Anacreontic Society, supported in its infancy by the Marquis of Donegal, would disappear in an amalgamation with the Belfast Philharmonic Society. On an aside, advertisements in the *Belfast Newsletter* in 1783 show that people were joining 'The Philharmonic Society'.

The Belfast 'Phil' met at the hall to rehearse, as did the Classical Harmonist Society (founded in 1851), so the uniting of all three was inevitable. However, back to happier days and that marvellous occasion on 26 March 1840. Admission was by ticket only; single tickets, 6s each (30p); family tickets to admit four, 21s (1 guinea).

The opening programme consisted of two parts. In the first part the leader was Mr Murray, with Mr Rudersdorf in the second, and Mr May conducting.

The concert began with the *Grand Overture To Anacreon* by Cherubin and concluded with the last movement of *Beethoven's Symphony in D*. There were pianoforte solos, flute and violin performances, vocal renditions and Miss Hayes' song *John Anderson My Joe*, and *Qui la Voce Sua Soave* by Bellini.

After that night Miss Hayes would return several times. Mr Murray's violin gave the packed house *Brilliant Variations* dedicated to Paganini, but little would Murray have believed that, on one of his several visits to the city, the maestro himself would drop in to attend a musical rehearsal.

Top performers in a wide variety of fields came to the May Street Music Hall. It was rarely used by 'variety turns' and was available for hire on a commercial basis. The music hall seems to have been used in much the same way as the present-day Ulster Hall, Kings Hall or Waterfront Hall. A festival celebration, a book or play reading, a classical concert or a solo performance—all had their place in May Street.

A few months after it opened, the Northern Horticultural Society held its summer show on Friday 12 June 1840. It was an event open to all, 'on payment of a small sum for each class'. The public competition was for 102 prizes. It cost one shilling to be admitted and children under twelve were given a 50 per cent reduction.

With its roots based in a music society, the emphasis was on classical music performances, especially in its early days, and these were almost always billed as a grand concert. Typical was a Grand Concert of Sacred Music on Thursday evening, 16 May 1842, with the works of Handel forming the main part of the programme.

There was a great variety of classical concerts, and on Wednesday 5 and Thursday 6 July 1848 there were the Baptist Lillo Concerts. Baptist Lillo, the juvenile vocalist, violinist and pianist, did the honour of announcing two grand concerts. He was assisted by his infant sister Minna Lillo, who was six years of age, named *L'enfant Rossignol*. She was to perform a concerto on the grand pianoforte.

On Tuesday evening, 13 March 1844, there was a Grand Vocal and International Concert, where the Band of the 13th Regiment, under the direction of Monsieur Gillaud from the Conservatoire de Paris, was to perform.

In stark contrast, on 19 June 1849, The Orange Band of the Belfast District gave a concert. The usual costs applied of 1 shilling to the body of the house and gallery; reserved seats were 6*d*; the platform was 2*s*, 6*d*.

Keeping in step with other venues, the music hall saw many Shakespearian readings and lectures on the board. On Monday 28 February and Friday 3 March, at the request of several friends, Mr Sheridan Knowles delivered two lectures on the 'Genius of Shakespeare'.

Among a host of others, Mrs Fanny Kemble gave lectures on the 'Three Readings of Shakespeare' across three days in the third week of May 1855, focusing on *Romeo and Juliet, A Winter's Tale* and *The Merchant of Venice*.

It comes, then, as no surprise that Shakespeare's tercentenary was acknowledged with 'a Grand Shakespearian Entertainment' in the music hall on Saturday evening, 23 April 1864.

The programme was very varied and included both readings and music. A few of the selections included *Who is Sylvia?*, *Hark the Lark!*, the third act of *Hamlet*, the fifth act of *The Merchant of Venice*, and an Irish ballad entitled *Ma Colleen Dheas Cruithe na Moe*. All were very reasonably priced at 1*s* 6*d* reserved, 1*s* for body of the hall and 6*d* for the gallery. Proceeds went to the Belfast Printers' Pension Society.

Three nights later the hall was hired out for a ball: 'Dancing at Nine for the Pupils and Friends of Mrs Lynch'. Tickets to admit a lady and a gentleman were 5 shillings. There were marionette shows to come, waxwork exhibitions, an evening of Scottish music, history, and song, and other entertainments.

The last advertisement that I could find appeared on Saturday 16 November 1872. It had run for a week, telling all who read it of the farewell tour and first and only appearance in Belfast of the wonderful 'Two-Headed Nightingale, Chrissie Millie'.

She was a lady who was bright and brilliant in conversation, highly educated, who sung solos

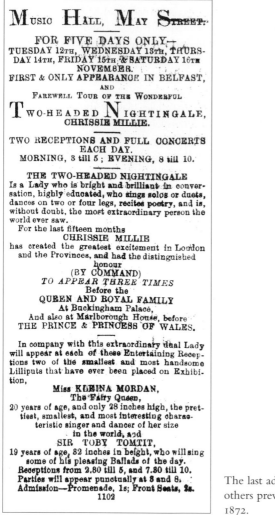

The last advertisement for May Street Music Hall. No others previous to this were found. Saturday 16 November 1872.

or duets, danced on two legs or four, and recited poetry. She was described as 'without doubt, the most extraordinary person the world ever saw'.

Chrissie Millie, the advertisement claims, appeared before the Queen and Royal family at Buckingham Palace and before other royalty elsewhere. Appearing with her were 'two of the smallest and most handsome lilliputs that have ever been put on exhibition'. These were Miss Kleina Morgan, the Fairy Queen, standing 28 inches tall and Sir Toby Tomtit, 32 inches in height. All this came at a cost of 1 shilling for the promenade and 2 shillings for the front seats.

It is impossible to leave the music hall without mentioning Daniel O'Connell, who visited a few days after his great Repeal meeting of 18 January 1841. He spoke from the Kearns Hotel balcony at the corner of Donegal Place. The following evening he attended a dinner in Batty's Circus on Chichester Street, where over eight hundred people dined.

It is reported that on Wednesday 20 January 'at 6 o'clock p.m. the doors of the music hall were opened and the large room was fitted up and lighted in brilliant style. At about half past six the whole of the company were assembled and there was a very pleasing display of well-dressed ladies. Upwards of 400 sat down to tea after Mr O'Connell's arrival' (Cathal O'Byrne). During tea, several stones were thrown through the window. After tea, Mr O'Connell, who presided, rose and led a toast to the Princess Royal, saying 'I hope she will emulate and imitate her mother and grandmother'. This was met with cheers.

Other toasts followed. The evening was a great success, but on the return to his hotel O'Connell was followed by stone throwing, hissing and booing.

The music hall eventually became known as the Victoria Memorial Hall in honour of Queen Victoria's Golden Jubilee. It had been taken over by the Church of Ireland's Young Men's Society. Eventually, in 1916, it was acquired by the Brethern Assembly. The hall was demolished in 1983.

Depending on which street directory one consulted, different addresses are given, but this is only a minor point for they were all the same location. In some, there is no reference to be found at all.

The fact that in 1868 the Church of England Young Men's Association is listed alongside it at 73 Upper Arthur Street, explains its natural acquisition of the hall in 1882. In 1852 it can be found at 42-60 Arthur Street Upper, and in 1870 its back entrance at 1 Music Hall Lane is the only reference found. All changes can easily be explained as new developments unfolded.

The Victoria Hall

The Victoria Hall opened in 1843 and was named after the reigning monarch. It was, unsurprisingly, located in Victoria Street, and was in the area named the 'Albert Buildings', comparatively close to Albert Square, where the landmark Albert Clock was built in the late 1860s. It is now a block of very expensive property.

The building is not listed in 1852 but appears in the *Belfast Street Directory of 1854*, and its porter was Joseph Mitchell. I could find no detailed description of the hall, but the 1879 directory gives details of the ground-floor housing a surveyor, an architect, and a civil engineer. The second floor holds the philharmonic room, but an advertisement of 12 September 1868 informs us that they were 'under the Victoria Hall'. In the 1858 directory it is stated that the entrance to the Victoria Hall, at 20 Victoria Street, is either by Victoria Street or Queen Square. Like May Street Music Hall, it seems to have been a multi-purpose hall and was available for hire. I could not find any reference to ownership.

As far as I am concerned, the first advertisement for the hall appeared on 11 January 1854. I looked particularly carefully prior to that date, but this was the only one that I found:

GRAND CONCERT
VICTORIA HALL, VICTORIA STREET
SAM COWELL'S RETURN TO IRELAND
For one night only
Wednesday 11 January

He was supported by Miss Austin, from the London and Liverpool Philharmonic Concerts, and Mr Warren, Professor of Music, Glasgow, on the grand pianoforte.

Cowell would have packed them in. His visit to the Shakespeare four years earlier saw hundreds turned away. In his earlier days he performed at Queen's Island and boosted the theatre variety image. He was a singer of comic songs and, although hailing from the northeast of England, was regarded as a Scot because his career began in Edinburgh. He was music hall's first star name.

A family ticket, to admit five, cost half a guinea, the gallery was 1s, the body of the hall was 1s 6d and, finally, reserved was 2s 6d (12 ½ p).

Over the years this type of music hall entertainment continued. Regular performers included Mr Charles du Val, the celebrated artiste, elocutionist, vocalist, mimic; Professor Anderson and his four daughters, who performed illusion and magic, and Poole and Young, who performed 'mystery, magic and mirth'.

There were many classical evenings. Catherine Hayes, who sang at the opening in May Street, gave two people's concerts on Saturday and Monday evenings, March 9 and 11, 1861.

It was used too for lectures and readings. The *Belfast Evening News* informed readers of a visit from Charles Dickens. On Friday evening, 27 August at 8 p.m., he was to read his *Christmas Carol*, followed by:

On Saturday August 28th at 3 o'clock, *The Story of Little Dombey*.

On Saturday evening, August 28th at 8 o'clock, *The Poor Traveller,*
Boots at the Hollytree Inn, and *Mrs Gamp.*

Places for Each Reading: Stalls (Numbered and Reserved)
Five Shillings; Unreserved Seats – half a crown
Back seats – 1 shilling

Earlier that year another well-known name appeared. This extract comes from an advertisement of 20 January 1858:

FOR A FEW DAYS ONLY
The Original and Celebrated American
GENERAL TOM THUMB
The Smallest Man in the World
Height 31 inches; Weight 25 lbs; Age 20 years

There are 3 entertainments a day
From 12 to 1 ½; 3 to 4 ½; 7 ½ to 9

The General will appear in all his characters, songs, dances, etc., including Napoleon,
Frederick the Great, Highlander, etc., etc.

Schools were 'liberally received' (was this the start of school educational visits?). During the day, admission was 1s; under 10 years, 6d. In the evening, reserved seats were 1s and children 6d. The General would return to the city on several occasions after this visit.

Where the Victoria Hall excelled was in showing Belfast's attempt at the moving pictures. Not the film version, but painted pictures on canvas, mounted on huge rollers, and placed at either side of the stage. By turning the rollers, the pictures were moved across the stage as the canvas unrolled. Music, vocal or instrumental, was chosen to complement the pictures. Credit for this format went to Dr T.C.S. Corry, who lived at the corner of Donegall Pass and Ormeau Road.

Cathal O'Byrne recorded that Dr Corry's entertainment was so successful that the owner and inventor travelled to the United States with it, after enjoying huge success all over Ireland, England and Scotland. It was called 'Dr Corry's "Diorama"'.

While several halls displayed such performances, the Victoria Hall easily led the field. The

QUAGLIENI'S NEW CIRQUE,
VICTORIA STREET, BELFAST.

MONDAY, APRIL 9,
Another grand change. Production of a new Grand
Equestrian Spectacle,

**BOLD ROBIN HOOD AND THE MERRY MEN
OF SHERWOOD FOREST; OR, THE EN-
CHANTED PRINCESS AND THE PRETTY
WHITE HORSE,**

Introducing the whole of the Company, aided by
auxiliaries, and the noble Stud of highly-trained
Horses.

All New Scenes in the Circle, displaying Elegant
and Refined Acts of Horsemanship, Calisthenics of a
high order, Icarian Games, Sports of Jupiter, and
Olympian Revels.

WEDNESDAY, April 11, Extra Night of Fun,
Fancy, Folly, and Frivolity, for the BENEFIT of
Mr. TOM FILLIS, Clown and Jester.

See special Bills.

FRIDAY, April 13, Grand Day Performance, commencing at 2.30. Bold Robin Hood and other
Amusements.

Admission—Stalls (select), 3s; Boxes (unreserved),
2s; Pit and Promenade, 1s; Gallery, 6d. Children
under Ten—Stalls, 2s; Boxes, 1s; Pit, 6d; Gallery, 6d.   695

Belfast Morning News,
9 April 1866.

HENGLER'S EQUESTRIAN PALACE,
VICTORIA STREET, BELFAST,

Open Every Evening at a Quarter-past SEVEN
o'clock, commencing at a Quarter to EIGHT, for a
short season only.

Day Performances every FRIDAY, by Gas-light,
and equal in every respect to the Evening Amusements. FRIDAY Evening, Fashionable Box Night,
by desire of several families of the *elite* of Belfast
and neighbourhood.

Every Evening during the Week, more Novelties!
more Attractions! more Wonders! more Exciting
Scenes by the Star Company of Equestrians.

DAVIS RICHARDS and JOHN HENRY COOKE
every Evening. A Grand Pageant, entitled KENIL-
WORTH, OR THE DAYS OF QUEEN ELIZABETH.
Tilting Match by Knights in Armour. BIBB'S Great
Ascent to the top of Gallery. The RIGS OF MR.
BRIGGS. Brilliant Entertainment. Mammoth
Establishment.

Prices of Admission—Stalls (Select), 3s.; Boxes, 2s.;
Pit, 1s.; Gallery, 6d. Children under Twelve years of
age, Half-price to Stalls, Boxes, and Pit. Second
Price at Nine o'clock to Stalls and Boxes only.

3294   CHARLES HENGLER, Proprietor.

Belfast Newsletter,
Friday 7 September 1860.

The first advertisement for Victoria Hall. *Belfast Newsletter*, 11 January 1854.

Belfast Newsletter, Monday 5 January 1890.

THE FRIENDLY ZULUS.

VICTORIA HALL.

TO-DAY AT 3.30,

FASHIONABLE LEVE.

EVENING AT 8, POPULAR CONCERT
AND LEVEE.

ON SATURDAY, MONDAY, AND TUESDA
At 8 o'clock only.

WAR SONGS AND DANCES.

WRESTLING, THROWING THE ASSEGA
AT A TARGET, FIGHTING WITH
ASSEGAI AND SHIELD.

The Hall is Nightly Crowded by highly re
ipectable and intelligent audiences.

Admission—2s, 1s, and 6d. Tickets at Cramei
Wood, & Co.'s.

The NEWS-LETTER says:—They are men o
ine physique and splendidly formed limbs.
n all their movements they displayed that agi
ity which can only be acquired by early an
ontinued physical exercise.

The Morning News says:—On the whole
ntertainment was in the highest degree interest.
ig, and we doubt not that many will flock to see
ie compatriots of those who have made for them.
lves such a figure in our military history. We
ere favoured with a personal interview with the
arriors, and they are, all of them, affable, manly,
id dignified fellows.

The Zulu Warriors were yesterday interviewed
7 several Gentlemen, one of whom (an eminent
iysician in Belfast) conversed with the men in
eir own language, and expressed himself satie-
d that they are

GENUINE ZULUS.
833

Belfast Newsletter,
Friday 25 July 1879.

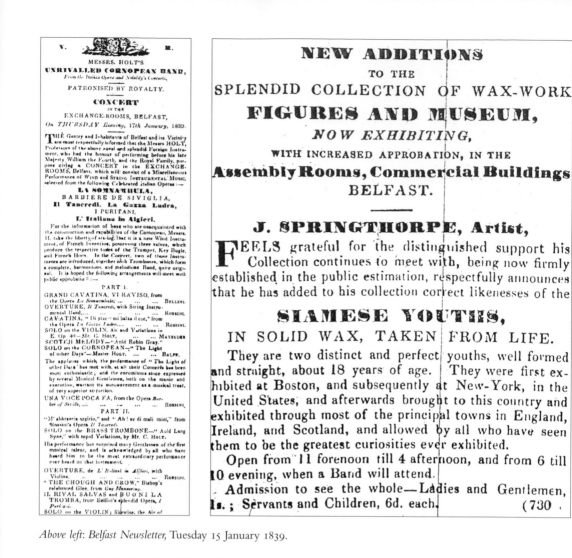

Above left: Belfast Newsletter, Tuesday 15 January 1839.

Above right: Belfast Newsletter, Wednesday 30 September 1837.

years 1854–1856 were those of the Crimean War and this is just one example of the very many advertisements published during that time. This one appeared on 14 August 1855.

NOW EXHIBITING

Mr Hampton's Grand Colossal Diorama
Illustrative of the
Wars of Napoleon
And the
Present Campaign in the Crimean
With the
Battles of Alma and Inkerman

Forty-Five Magnificent Tableaux
Painted by … Mr Charles Marshal, for her Majesty's
Italian Opera and a host of Talented Artists
Later … W.H. Edward's Great Panorama of the
War in America and Wandering in the Far West
(with appropriate songs, anecdotes and music).

In 1863 a series of advertisements placed throughout September indicated the imminent closure of Victoria Hall. 'Will close soon', announced the first, followed by 'Victoria Hall definitely closing'. Finally, in the third week of the month, 'Victoria Hall will close on Friday 20 September'. And that was that.

Some time later, during another search, I came across the hall again, as large as life. Its new career had begun perhaps a month after closure, and normal service was resumed with a potpourri of variety shows, concerts and 'diorama' presentations.

The Four Corners

In the overall picture, a quick visit to Belfast's Four Corners is a must. It was, and still is, the historic centre of Belfast, where North Street, Bridge Street and Rosemary Street converge. For a time, distance was measured from this junction.

The important buildings, still there today, were in great demand. A third, the Corn Exchange, was nearby and was variously described as being the first or last house in either Corporation Street or Victoria Street. Knowing their historical background casts them in a different light today.

First we come to the Northern Bank building, known as the Exchange. Built in 1769, and added to in 1776, it became the Assembly Rooms in 1769 with its address as 2 Waring Street. It was a Charles Lanyon building where the Irish Harpers met in July 1792.

Fifty years after its opening, on St Patrick's Day 1819, the Marquis of Donegall laid the foundation stone of the Commercial Buildings. Today it is the Northern Whig Building at 1-3 Waring Street and it too had Assembly Rooms. Next to it was Widow Partridge's Inn.

The *Belfast Street Directory of 1813* states 'The Exchange/Assembly Rooms, Commercial Buildings, Corn Exchange, is situated at the termination of Waring Street, Donegall Street, North Street and Bridge Street. The building is handsome and light, of brick partially faced with stone. Above are elegant Assembly Rooms and below a piazza where merchants assemble on Monday at 12, Wednesday at 12 and Friday at 11 to transact business.'

The Assembly Rooms staged wide-ranging cultural and social events. Operatic evenings were frequent, perhaps with music from *The Barber of Seville* or *The Italian Girl in Algiers*, and instrumental performers.

The public crowded in to see for themselves such exhibitions as 'Groves' Elegant Exhibition of Mechanical Ingenuity' (in November 1838), 'Superb Animated Spectacles—the Departure of the Children of Israel for Egypt'; 'The City of London—The Tower, St Paul's, etc., etc., with animated figures' and 'The Grand Naval View of the Storming of Algiers'. The Exchange was also quick to join other venues in 'diorama' displays.

In March 1838 it displayed a new panorama, of which there were six showings daily:

The Holy City of Jerusalem
And surrounding county of Judea as far as the Dead Sea
The Mountains of Arabia

Valley of Jehosaphat, Mount of Slaves

Etc etc etc.

Painted from drawings made on the spot from the terrace or roof of the AGA, or Governor's
House, formerly the Palace of Pontius Pilate

Daily at 1, 2, 3 and 7, 8, 9 o'clock.

Other screenings included *The Celebrated Panorama of New York, Napoleon Bonaparte Crossing the Alps, The Beautiful City of Venice*, and so on. There was little that could be called variety music hall.

Where the Commercial Buildings (Northern Whig) now stands, there was previously a row of thatched cottages. Like its neighbour opposite, it had regular shows. In both instances I have only scanned the newspaper columns to satisfy myself that both deserve a mention, and to prove their existence and contribution.

I formed the opinion that the Commercial Buildings' events were for smaller audiences, but I can't be certain. Here are a few examples of what could be seen and heard.

On Friday 21 December 1832 those attending would have listened to Mr and Mrs Woods, 'celebrated vocalists of the Theatres Royal Drury Lane and Covent Garden'. This was typical entertainment, while in September 1835 they queued to visit a 'Splendid Waxworks Exhibition' which featured 'Siamese youths' as its main attraction.

Those with free time on Thursday 31 August and Friday 1 September were urged to come and listen to Professor William Barry, 'the celebrated pianist', whose writings obtained for him the appellation of the 'Beethoven of Ireland', and hear him perform 'two grand *soirees*'.

Nearby, up at the corner of Albert Square, stood the Corn Exchange, founded in 1851 by the corn merchants of Belfast. Like the previous two, the programme offered was very similar. Again, I have included the names of a few to illustrate the range.

Three distinguished Scottish vocalists gave four concerts in February 1856. They were not named but their programme advertisement read:

On Monday Feb. 11: A Nicht wi' Burns,

On Tuesday Feb 12: Adventures of Prince Charles in 1745,

On Wednesday Feb 13: A Land O' Cakes,

On Thursday 14: Wanderin' Willies Wallet.

Totally different was Signor Pompei, buffo singer and oboe player, whose classical programme, complete with a full cast, commenced on Tuesday 16 March 1858, and lasted for a week.

Over the years Belfast seems to have had a fascination with quirky shows. Real Red Indians, General Tom Thumb, Bedouin Arabs. A one-legged prize packet and genuine slaves. Biggest, smallest, lightest, heaviest. Think of an attraction that would have been an oddity at the time and you could see it in downtown Belfast.

Opening in the first week of January 1864, and appearing for four nights, was Monsieur Brice, 'The Largest Man in the World', and he certainly was a front-runner as the newspaper description proclaimed. 'This modern Goliath is eight feet high, thirty stones in weight and only twenty-three years old'. No mention is made of his shoe size.

The advertisement carried the information 'The Hall is held select for the elite of Belfast from two till five o'clock, and those who honour his Highness with their presence at that time will avoid the unpleasant crushing which always takes place in the evenings.'

Belfast's Early Theatres

When it came to 'the Stage', Belfast lagged behind Dublin, which played host to court theatricals in the reign of Elizabeth I and could boast of a public theatre as early as 1635. Unlike the Dublin scene, there are no records of Belfast's earliest theatre days.

It is not until 18 June 1731 that there is a hint of early theatre in the town. Even this evidence is scarce. However, absolutely without dispute is the entry in the register of the first Presbyterian church in Rosemary (Street) Lane, indicating the burial of a 'Mrs Johnes'. The entry reads 'June 18, Mrs Johnes, playhouse'.

The custom of the time means that this was the locality from which the funeral moved off, or in which the deceased resided. Again, at the time, the use of 'playhouse' does indicate somewhere 'befitting to proper performances, having proper form and ceremony'. Could it have been the Market House or somewhere more formal in structure, more dedicated to theatre productions?

This early record establishes the fact that there was provision for theatre prior to 1731, but no one seems the wiser as to the location of that particular 'playhouse'. It is also clear from the early writing and books on the subject, that there were informal theatres around, where strolling players performed on trestle structures, set up to form a stage in any available space.

No record remains of this, probably because in the absence of newspapers, advertising was through playbills posted in public places, or announced via a drummer parading around like a town crier, or no doubt relayed by word of mouth.

Elsewhere in the late eighteenth century, there were often private theatres in large private town and country houses that engaged companies to come and perform. One such venue was in Shane's Castle, where Mrs Sarah Siddons, the leading actress of the period, was an enthusiastic visitor during the summer of 1784 after an acting engagement in Dublin. It was described as 'an elegant theatre'.

Over the next one hundred years, Belfast's entertainment scene developed, with recognised theatres and music halls at named locations, but before going along that road I'm going to leap forward to the mid-nineteenth century, for by 1850 there were numerous smaller, but nevertheless important, Belfast theatres.

Smithfield Square was a busy place. Not only did it have a public house on each corner and several others as well, but a number of theatres. Nearby in North Street there seems to have been another theatre. Exactly where I don't know, but several references to it exist.

Back in 'The Square' stood number 44½. If it were there today it would be found by exiting the rear doors of Castle Court and going straight ahead towards North Street.

The centre of the Square was essentially an open space for trading and, having read a number of accounts, I am still not certain of the actual number of theatres there, but the first at 44½ is a certainty.

Heffernon's National Theatre was there, and when the Central Picture House was being built in 1913 the report stated, 'it is a conversion of an existing premise' and named the National, which was open by 1849. In 1858 Mrs Armitage was listed in the street directory as its proprietor, and by 1852 it was a Thomas Armitage, but the references end in 1863.

Away across the open space I tracked down the source of references to our Hibernian Theatre. Like its rival it was going strong by 1849, with 14 Smithfield Square as its address.

I wondered if I should consider it a music hall, for its title in 1852 was 'The Royal Hibernian Concert Hall'. Had the proprietors moved with the times and changed direction? If so, it was short-lived, for the site was vacant by 1858.

Various references show that a third was McCormick's Theatre. I failed to trace it to an exact location but feel it was later than the National and the Hibernian. Further, there is a 'vagueness' regarding an unnamed building (perhaps a mysterious fourth?) but I couldn't resolve it, so now back to the middle of the eighteenth century.

Belfast's first recorded theatrical performance took place in 1736 when the Smock Alley Company, managed by Louis Duvall, came to town at the end of the Dublin season, and it was to return again and again during the course of the eighteenth century.

The company opened on 16 July with *The Comedy of the Stratagem*. Their stay was short and they returned in October. For such a well-known company, one likely venue was the Market House, where they had originally performed.

Although there are references made in writings of the period, the first traceable advertisement appears in the *Belfast Newsletter* of Tuesday 2 January 1749.

As in so many advertisements in those early years, no venue is given, but those attending are informed that the performance 'is to begin at exactly 6 o'clock'. The name of the venue is missing so often that the only conclusion that can be drawn is that there were so few options that patrons knew the location.

The advertisement read:

BY PERMISSION OF THE WORSHIPFUL, THE SOVERIGN OF BELFAST
On Wednesday the 3rd of January
(For the benefit of Mr Duncan and Miss Quinn)
will be acted a tragedy called the
LONDON MERCHANT
Or the history of George Boswell

Although no location is mentioned, the date indicates that it was most likely staged in the Vaults in Ann Street or in the already mentioned Market House. They would have had a proper theatre in Dublin and probably expected no less in Belfast.

An advertisement in the *Belfast Newsletter* on 13 April 1795 places the Vaults in Ann Street, as Francis and John Turnly announce in the property column:

TO LET – THAT WELL-SITUATED TENEMENT IN WEIGH HOUSE LANE,
denominated The Old Vaults with stores therein

Weigh House Lane ran alongside St George's Church towards Ann Street, and was demolished in 1849 to create a new street, to be named after the monarch, Queen Victoria, who visited the town on 11 August 1849.

From around 1750, Belfast's theatre scene advanced in huge strides. Much in the same way as the Smithfield area was a centre for the stage in the 1850s period, so the area around present-day Bridge Street/Ann Street became the focal point of the 1750s. One man in particular dominated for fifty years. His name was Michael Atkins.

Michael Atkins was a colossus in terms of what he achieved, and ranks alongside the better-known theatrical names of Willie Ashcroft, Dan Lowrey or John J. Stamford—men more of the music hall theatre than the stage—and the lesser-known E.M. Heffernon of not only the National Theatre in Smithfield Square, but of another in Lodge Road in 1860. Heffernon was also proprietor of the Queen's Theatre, Londonderry.

An 1868 advertisement of 20 August tells us that the theatre on Lodge Road was open every evening at 7 p.m., with admission prices in the stalls for 1s, the pit for 6d and the gallery, 3d.

For his performance with 'an efficient, dramatic company', his prospective audiences had to 'see day bills for particulars', once more to be found on street advertisements.

Now that Atkins is in town, it's time to move on to Belfast's 'Big Five' and the Dubliner associated with all of them as they span the second half of the nineteenth century. In order, the Big Five are the Vaults, the Mill Gate, New Theatre Ann Street, Rosemary Lane and the Theatre, eventually the Theatre Royal, Arthur Square.

The Vaults and New Theatre were in the Ann Street area, the Mill Gate up towards Millfield, while the Rosemary Lane Play House was right there, opposite the church. It must be remembered that the Market House was also operating at this time.

Such was the contribution of Atkins that, had circumstances permitted it, there is no doubt that he would have been placed in a situation where he would have been confronted by Eamonn Andrews or Michael Aspel, and shown the 'Big Red Book'. 'Michael Atkins—Theatre Actor, Theatre Manager—this is your life!'

Atkins was not only a jack of all trades, but was also master of all.

The Market House 1639 - 1810

When Michael Atkins stepped off the post-chaise at No. 10 Castle Place and looked around him, his eye would undoubtedly have lit upon the Market House on the corner of High Street and Cornmarket.

The Dubliner would have been one of the early travellers on what was a very recent service linking Belfast and Dublin and, appropriately, given his career to come, he alighted practically on the doorstep of the town's first building, the town hall and theatre.

Built in 1639, with a floor added in 1663, it was the main public hall of the town and records show that it was well used and popular with actors and entertainers alike. It is more than possible that it was a playhouse of the late Mrs Johnes, who died and was buried from Rosemary Street church on 18 June 1731.

An appearance from leading actress Sarah Siddons established the Market House as a venue featuring some of the best performers. In 1783, a Mrs McTier, who had been watching Siddons act, wrote to her brother in Dublin that 'her acting was so powerful that in the last act of *The Unhappy Marriage*, ladies were taken out fainting and hardly a man could stand it.'

The Market House must be regarded as the town's first official theatre and music hall. Perhaps the demise of Mrs Johnes helped to establish its credentials. If not, an advertisement in the *Belfast Newsletter* in May 1756 does:

> For The Benefit Of The Distressed
> At the Market House
> On Thursday next, being 20th inst.
> Will be acted a comedy called
> The Recruiting Officer

Even at this early date, its contribution to grass-roots music hall had begun, and the first record of a variety show duly noted, although no exact date was put to an act that several authors wrote was billed as a 'first for Europe'.

On that particular occasion the Market House's doors opened at 5 p.m. with the performance commencing at 7 p.m. To keep the intended audiences entertained, a Monsieur Dominic 'balanced by an arm on the back of a chair'. Surely not for the whole two hours! Whatever else it happened to be, it was a music hall type of act.

Now we come to a real variety show. On Monday 21 October 1754 a *Belfast Newsletter* advertisement declared:

> In the Market House, a celebrated company of rope dancers and tumblers will
> perform. Balances on a slack wire by Mr Barbarous.
> Price 1s,1d. Doors open at five, begins precisely at seven o'clock.

The Market House tradition, supported by events in the 'pubs and clubs' of that time, was the background against which Michael Atkins put his stamp on the Belfast theatre scene.

Whatever part the Market House played in establishing early theatre and music hall, it served as a town hall for 150 years before being demolished in 1812. The new town hall was located at 23 Castle Place for ten years.

Now we join Atkins in the mid-1760s as he sets about establishing himself in Belfast, beginning a career that will span forty years.

The Vaults 1749 - 1769

Although there is no direct proof that Michael Atkins performed at the Vaults, the circumstantial evidence is very strong. The date of his arrival is uncertain, but later references in his Mill Gate Theatre days make it clear that he had already been involved in 'theatre' in Belfast. Realistically, where else could that have been other than the Vaults?

As the Turnly advertisement of 13 April 1795 proves, the Vaults was located in a tenement building in Weigh House Lane, closer to Ann Street than the St George's end. As to when it opened, no precise date can be found, but I feel that it is safe to say it would have been prior to 1749. Circumstantial evidence places it at that time.

In the eighteenth century, companies and performers seemed to have a continuing connection with a particular theatre. Although I failed to spot an advertisement for the Smock Alley Theatre Company appearing at the Vaults, others recorded their presence. They first came in 1736 and subsequently many times, so there is a fair chance that the Vaults was the venue earlier than the assumed 1749 date.

After the first theatre advertisement of Tuesday 2 January 1749, there was no trumpeting of a special opening occasion anywhere. The play, a tragedy called *London Merchant*, would have required proper staging and I feel that it would not have been in the Market House which had a foot in each camp, staging drama, and music hall, plus acting as a public building.

In December 1751, the Royal Company of Comedians, from the theatres of London and Dublin, performed there. Incredibly, two playbills of the time survive in the Harvard Theatre Collection at the University's Houghton Library. How they came to rest there would be a story in itself. They were most likely carried safely, for they are in mint condition, by someone emigrating who was closely associated with the Vaults, and took them as reminders of their time spent there.

They provide proof of the Vault's existence and its type of programme. While only one playbill is dated, they are undoubtedly of the same period, as the performers are the same and the leading

By a Company of COMEDIANS from the THEATRES of LONDON and DUBLIN.

G.   II.R.

At the VAULTS in BELFAST.

ON *Monday* Evening, will be Presented, A COMEDY, call'd,

The Merry WIVES of WINDSOR.

(Written by *Shakespear*.)

The Part of Sir *JOHN FALSTAFF*, by *Mr.* LOVE.

Sir *HUGH EVANS*, by *Mr.* LEWIS.

SLENDER, by *Mr.* GEMEA.

Mr. Ford,		Mr. Phillipson.		Simple,		Mr. Bushby.
Mr. Page,	by	Mr. Brown.		Rugby,	by	Master Sennet.
Host,		Mr. Tyrer.		Robin,		Master Lewis.
Fenton,		Mr. Howard.		Anne Page,		Mrs. Love.

JUSTICE SHALLOW, by *Mr.* P. LEWIS.

The Part of Doctor *CAIUS*, by *Mr.* GUITAR.

Mrs. QUICKLY, by *Mrs.* GEMEA.

Mrs. PAGE, by *Mrs.* TYRER.

And the Part of *Mrs. FORD*, by *Mrs.* LEWIS.

With a FARCE, call'd,

The Honest YORKSHIRE-MAN.

The Part of *GAYLOVE*, by *Mr.* LEWIS.

SAPSCULL, by *Mr.* TYRER.

Muckworm,	by	Mr. P. Lewis.		Blunder,	by	Mr. Love.
Slango,		Mr. Gemeo.		Servant,		Mr. Bushby.

COMBRUSH, by *Mrs.* GEMEA.

And the Part of *ARABELLA*, by *Mrs.* LOVE.

Pit 2 *s.* 2 *d.* Gallery 1 *s.* 1 *d.*   To begin exactly at Seven o'Clock

TICKETS to be had at Mr. LOVE's Lodgings at Mrs. Gibson's, in *Forest's* Lane; and at the Crown.

N. B. *No Children or Servants will be admitted without paying.*

N. B. It is hoped, NO GENTLEMAN will attempt to come behind the CURTAIN, or into the Dressing Room this Night, on any Account whatever; the Play being so extremely full of Business, that it but the Presence of a SINGLE PERSON behind the Scenes must greatly disconcert the Repr...

This is a scan of the original bill, courtesy of the Houghton Library, Harvard University.

actor was Mr. P. Love, strangely supported by Mr. P. Lewis. Both gentlemen appear again and again when the company visits.

The theatre was flourishing, and, given its uncertain starting date, it probably had a lifespan of around twenty years.

I have selected a few advertisements to quote from, which will give an indication of its programme, starting with the *Belfast Newsletter* advertisement of 1 June 1753. Three leading actors of the time featured in the play *The Mourning Bride* with Tom Thumb the Great to follow. Mr and Mrs Sherriff and Mr Lewis returned time and time again. Lewis had already featured in the 1751 productions.

The Vaults was now clearly well established on the theatre circuit. There was a change of programme weekly in the summer of 1753, with performances on Monday, Wednesday and Friday evenings. This was the common practice of the period.

The season was a mix of the serious and more light-hearted and ended on 7 September with a comedy entitled *The Careless Husband*, which was a benefit for Mrs Sherriff.

On 3 January 1755 the Vaults staged Belfast's first pantomime, a production of *Harlequin Animated*, which followed its production of *The Conscious Lover*.

There always seemed to be two plays, rather like the time in the cinema when there was a 'Big Picture' and a B-rated movie. In the first week of January 1766, the theatre staged King Richard III and on Friday 28 February, *Hamlet, Prince of Denmark*, in the 150th anniversary year of the Bard's death. The evening concluded with 'a New Ballad Farce-The Humours of Belfast'.

Below is the text from two advertisements for the Vaults. In some parts, the text was too dark and illegible to make out the words.

At the Vaults on Wednesday next (never before here) will be presented a Tragedy call'd
MOURNING BRIDE, the part of ... by Mr. Sherriff, H. ... by Mr Lewis and the
part of Athenia by Mrs Sherriff. With a farce call'd
Tom Thumb the Great

Belfast Newsletter, 1 June 1753

(Positively the last night of performing)

For the benefit of Mrs Berry
At The Vaults in Belfast
By a company of comedians
On Monday next, being the 10th of March 1766
Will be presented a comedy call'd
THE INCONSTANT
Or the
WAY TO WIN HIM

To which will be added (by particular desire) a farce call'd, What We Must All Come To

Belfast Newsletter, 10 March 1766

The Mill Gate 1768 - 1788

There is no doubt in my mind that the New Theatre in Millfield brought about the Vaults' demise. The public are fickle and a new, contemporary building would no doubt draw the audiences away

...y the **COMEDIANS** from the **THEATRES** of *LONDON* and *DUBLIN*.

At the VAULTS in BELFAST.

ON *Wednesday*, the Eighteenth Day of *December*, 1751, will be Presented,
A TRAGEDY, call'd,

JANE SHORE.

The Part of Lord *HASTINGS*, by Mr. LOVE.

GLOSTER, by Mr. GEMEA.

Catesby, ⎱ by ⎰ Mr. Tyrer. ‖ Earl of Derby, ⎱ by ⎰ Mr. Phillipson.
Ratcliffe, ⎰ ⎱ Mr. Brown. ‖ Porter, ⎰ ⎱ Mr. Bushby.

BELLMOUR, by Mr. P. LEWIS.

The Part of *SHORE*, by Mr. LEWIS.

ALICIA, by Mrs. GEMEA.

And the Part of *JANE SHORE*, by Mrs. LEWIS.

With Entertainments of Singing between the Acts, by *Mrs.* LOVE.
Particularly,
End of Act 2d,---*Go, Rose, &c.*
End of Act 4th,---*The Highland Laddie*; new set by *Master* Arne.

With a FARCE, call'd,

The VIRGIN UNMASK'D.

The Part of *GOODWILL*, by *Mr.* P. LEWIS.
BLISTER, by Mr. LEWIS.

Coupee, ⎱ by ⎰ Mr. Tyrer. ‖ Wormwood, ⎱ by ⎰ Mr. Gemea.
Quaver, ⎰ ⎱ Mr. Love. ‖ Mr. Thomas, ⎰ ⎱ Mr. Bushby.

And the Part of Miss *LUCY*, by Mrs. LOVE.

Pit 2 s. 2 d. Gallery 1 s. 1 d.   To begin exactly at Seven o'Clock.

TICKETS to be had at of LOVE's Lodgings at the *Crown*.

This is a scan of the original bill, courtesy of the Houghton Library, Harvard University.

from an older one. With the closure of the Vaults, the spotlight shifted to Mill Gate.

The Mill Gate Company was founded by a man called Parker, who opened his theatre in a blaze of glory on 12 August 1768. He enjoyed outstanding publicity that praised the Mill's luxury, although the building is not thought to have been very imposing. Throughout its early life, the Mill Gate enjoyed the patronage of the Donegall family, which meant that it must have been quite prestigious, living up to its press reports. However, towards the end it was struggling, and it eventually bowed out in late 1788 or early 1789.

It is the first-night production on 13 August that finally gives us proof that Michael Atkins was already an experienced actor and was probably arriving from the nearby Vaults.

By Command of the Right Honorable the Countess of Donegall
at the New Theatre in Mill Street.

By Comedians from the Theatre Royal at London,
Dublin and Edinburgh.

This present evening, being 13th August 1768,
will be presented

THE BEGGARS' OPERA

To which will be added The MILLER OF MANITOBA
King: Mr Atkins. Miller: Mr Walsh. Kate: Mrs Pye. Peggy: Mrs Maxwell.
To begin at seven o'clock. No patron whatsoever will be admitted behind the scenes.

Atkins remained with the company until things took a downward turn. He must still have been quite young then (for a forty-year career lies ahead of an actor who begins his stage career at seventeen) and he would go on to become a theatre manager and celebrity.

One location for the Mill Gate has been given as close to Smithfield, between North Street and Castle Street, but I found it referenced on an early map. Curiously, it precedes the advertised opening of August 1768 and is located, in today's terms, as being at 4, 6, 8 Mill Street, which would be on the upper corner of Queen Street and Castle Street. That map is dated 1767. I double-checked but my information seems to hold up. Perhaps it was just being built.

Historically, Mill Gate was one of three gates in the fortified walls of Belfast and was almost exactly where the main road intersects Castle Street and the start of the Falls Road. The others were North Gate, where Royal Avenue crosses, and Strand Gate, close to the present Custom House.

Three weeks after the opening, Atkins stepped out from the wings as the lead in *Romeo and Juliet* but for the time being his real ambitions were on hold as he became heavily involved in all aspects of theatre-life.

He was a jack of all trades and must have been invaluable to the management, which had changed from Parker to a Mr Ryder on 3 April 1770, premiering with *The Suspicious Husband* and *The Mock Doctor*. Atkins was a stage hand, a first-class artist, a scenery painter and a general handyman, but he was primarily an actor. Performing with the indefatigable Atkins at Mill Gate was one Myrton Hamilton. Both were 'going places' in the profession and would become theatre managers. Atkins' debut as a theatre manager was at Rosemary Lane, followed by the New Theatre in Arthur Square. Hamilton's was at the Theatre in Ann Street.

A strong, philanthropic vein ran through Belfast's early theatre and society of that time, an example of which was the early 'Market House Benefit for the Distressed' on 20 May 1756. The

Mill Gate hosted its first charity evening on 20 January 1769.

> The company at Mill Gate will give a Benefit to the
> Poor. Pit and Gallery 2s 2d each. The Sovereign (Lord Mayor) will attend to take the tickets.

This was obviously the equivalent of a black-tie evening and was a 'come and be seen' occasion.

When Mr Ryder assumed control he was determined to go upmarket and 'raise the tone'. His theatre advertisement describes at length 'the propriety and decorum which the manager is resolved to observe' and lists the house regulations.

He follows established practices and opens on Monday, Wednesday and Friday, which begs the question, what entertainment was being provided on the other evenings? It is also important to note that even the cheapest prices were extremely costly when translated into flagons of ale at 1d per fill. Meanwhile, a rousing and less costly night could be had in the emerging inns and taverns where music and singing were on offer.

The first stirrings of music hall were underway, with the more formal development yet to emerge. For the working class, there was still value for money and a good time on offer.

Twice in the early 1770s Ryder ran into problems. On 15 July 1771, the *Belfast Newsletter* reports that 'the theatre in Mill Street is repairing and will reopen in a few days'. On 14 November 1775, this is echoed following reports of necessary repairs.

> The theatre in Mill Street will open in a few days with a play and a farce as will be expressed
> in the Bills. A few free tickets for the theatre will be disposed of transferable at a guinea and a
> half each (£1.57) to be had of Mr Atkins.

Interestingly, below this advertisement is one for a theatre in Lisburn where *Richard III* was being performed with the crime opera *Padlock*.

The decline of 'the old house in Mill Street' seemed to set in from February 1775. It was occupied by a performer, equilibrist and wire-walker by the name of Bissett, but it rallied to regain some stature.

It appears to have been the setting for Sheridan's masterpiece *The School for Scandal*, which was a premiere for the town. Again, as happens so often, there was no clearly stated venue but, as Atkins is there, it is short odds that it is Mill Gate. However, from the mid-1780s it was struggling. Atkins and Hamilton had long since departed to pastures new, but the Dubliner would be sorry to see it described in print (1788) as 'being a disgrace to the town'. Closure came no later that 1789. There were other theatres, but all were more casual, temporary, or short-lived and none had a permanent manager.

It is worth noticing at this time that a Mr Bellerton, or Ballerton, built 'another theatre' in Hill Street, which prompts the question, which other one did he build and where?

Two advertisements of this time point out Belfast's Choral tradition. On 19 October 1768 the *Newsletter* carried this announcement from the Belfast Musical Society.

> On Friday November 4th, being the anniversary of the birth of King William of
> Glorious and Immortal Memory, there will be a concert of vocal and instrumental music,
> after which there will be a ball at Mr Brackley's Long Room for the benefit of the Poor
> Reduced Housekeepers of the Town of Belfast.

'Theatre, Belfast' here is referring to the Mill Gate Theatre. This ad appeared in the *Belfast Newsletter*, 28 January 1774.

In 1783, I spotted a reference to people joining the Philharmonic Society. Frustratingly, I failed to make out the date.

Ann Street 1778 - 1792

If anyone is still in doubt that Michael Atkins had what it takes to go all the way, read on. The mover and shaker of early Belfast theatre stepped away from Mill Gate as he saw it decline, as did Myron Hamilton. Maybe they even planned it together, for both took up residence at the New Theatre in Ann Street, albeit, in the case of Atkins, for a relatively short time.

The new venture failed to live up to his expectations after his departure from Mill Street in 1778. One source notes that Ann Street Theatre was its replacement, but as we have seen, this was not the case, as it limped along for a decade more.

Atkins' last role there was as Lord Hastings in *Jane Shore*, a favourite play of the time, performed on Friday 10 April. At that time he was the star of the ailing Mill Gate, and after joining forces with Hamilton, he left the Mill short of two dynamic personalities, who, had they stayed, might just have turned it around.

Ann Street opened on either 23 or 28 October 1778, and by tradition was sited in the corner of Upper Church Street Lane and Ann Street, with its advertisements always headed 'Theatre— Ann Street'. Their patron was the town's sovereign, George Black, whose name appeared frequently in connection with the productions.

The managerial role seems to have fallen to Hamilton. Atkins' career was moving forwards but it was Hamilton who was the first to go on stage at the new venue.

In 1865 A.S. Black described the successful launch and the opening event of Friday 23 October, but I failed to find this in the *Belfast Newsletter*. A careful search produced the first advertisement in the Tuesday 27 October edition.

I have a sneaking suspicion that the sovereign George Black and A.S. Black may have been related, and that the author was perhaps quoting from an original playbill. His version is the only one that I have ever come across that simply read 'Theatre-Belfast'. Each and every other bill always added 'Ann Street'. In spite of that I'm putting the opening date down as Friday 23 October 1778. Here are the two notices:

THEATRE BELFAST

By Permission of the Worshipful George Black esq.,
Sovereign of Belfast (By the Comedians)

This present evening Friday 23 October 1778
The New Theatre in Ann Street
Will be opened by a prologue.

Written by a gentleman of Belfast to be spoken
(in the character of a sailor) by Mr Hamilton.
After which (not acted here these ten years) the comedy

RUN A WIFE and HAVE A WIFE

THEATRE ANN STREET

By Permission of the Worshipful George Black esq.,
(By the Belfast Comedians)

On Wednesday evening 28th October will (*have*)
Presented the comedy of the
STRATAGEM
To which will be added the Farce

HONITON
Or High Life above station

The theatre put on a continuous programme of the usual mix of comedy, farce and tragedy for the next five years, but at that stage all was not well in Ann Street.

One source tells that 'the Old House in Ann Street is in poor condition and needing an artistic overhaul'. A second opinion described it as 'small, infirm and inconvenient'. Atkins had seen it all before.

Quite clearly, he was disenchanted. His itchy feet were telling him it was time to move on to greener pastures. However, this time there was a difference, for he was going to do his own thing and be his own master. So he took a decisive action and the result was a massive fall-out between himself and Hamilton.

At the time, the *Newsletter* appeared on Tuesdays and Fridays. The publication of Tuesday 7 June to Friday 10 June 1783 carried an acknowledgement to an appeal made in April by Atkins for subscriptions to enable him to purchase a plot of land—'now achieved Rosemary Lane'—to erect a new theatre. I looked for the original but the print was so black as to be illegible.

The site he chose is opposite the First Presbyterian Church in Rosemary Street (then Rosemary Lane) and the foundation stone was laid at the end of the theatre season in 1783, the same year that the White Linen Hall was built.

Hamilton must have got wind of the 'thank-you' notice, for alongside it is his response. In it, he is proposing to enlarge and improve his building and seeks contributions. This action shows that at least the earlier continued to operate for some time.

However, Atkins did better as Rosemary Lane proves. The advertisement in the paper read 'Mr Atkins takes this method of relating his thanks to those respectable gentlemen who have honoured me with a subscription to his New Theatre.' Again, a source claims Rosemary Street opened to replace 'a theatre', presumably Ann Street, but this was actually not so.

The clock was ticking for Atkins and Hamilton. Atkins had the money in the bank. The foundation stone had been laid. The Play House, Rosemary Lane, was about to become a reality, but Hamilton's dream was all but over.

In 1788 George Benn found an advertisement stating that 'The Theatre in Ann Street must be enlarged' but he went on to describe it as 'being levelled in 1792'.

Rosemary Lane 1784 - 1793

NEW THEATRE, BELFAST
On Wednesday evening the 3rd instant will be presented the celebrated comedy of

THE WEST INDIAN

To which will be added the Musical Entertainment of
THE SON-IN-LAW

Prices to the boxes 3s 3d; Pit 2s 2d; Gallery 1s 1d.

Belfast Newsletter, 3 March 1784

Up until this point, whatever his accomplishments or his input elsewhere, Michael Atkins had nevertheless only been a hired hand. Rosemary Lane changed all that. Here he was master in his own house. It had been his focus in his appeal for funding to realise his dream. It opened on Wednesday 3 March 1784. Unimaginatively, he dropped 'play house', and 'Rosemary Lane' became yet another 'New Theatre'.

The Play House had its front door in Rosemary Lane, a few doors down from Hercules Street (Royal Avenue), on the opposite side from the Rosemary Street Presbyterian Church. Its players might well have lodged in the Donegall Arms Hotel, which was certainly operating by 1786 and was sited where the former Bewley's Coffee Shop was at the end of Donegall Arcade. By 1788, but possibly much earlier, the hotel had its own 'Little Theatre', as an advertisement of 11 January of that year shows.

Atkins had not actually purchased a plot of land, but had taken a lease for part of the rear garden of a genteel dwelling house in Grand Parade (Chichester Street). This stretched all the way back to Rosemary Lane. The acquisition contained 'sufficient ground on which a small square might be built', although this never materialised.

In today's terms this seems impossible, and, even then, maps show Castle Lane and High Street cutting across. Obviously the owner must have been owner of all the land stretching back.

Later in its life, its description as the old wooden theatre in Rosemary Lane gives us an indication of its construction. It took approximately six months to build. Although it closed in 1793, the building was still there when a map, dated from 1797, was produced. A laneway ran back from Rosemary Lane itself with the directions 'To our Old Playhouse' included.

The entrepreneur set himself high standards and was determined that his audiences would have only the best. He brought the big names of the acting profession to Rosemary Lane. His advertisement in the *Newsletter*, that ran from Friday 26 until Thursday 30 September 1786, was written in the style of the period and is worth setting out in full.

> Mr Atkins, happy to embrace every means of convincing the polite and liberal audience of Belfast, of his gratitude and respect, has engaged the celebrated Mrs Ashmel the … female eminent of the Irish stage (a lady possessed of the most uncommon abilities) for a number of nights.

> He also engaged that most excellent comedian Mr Lee Lewes from the Theatre Royal, Covent Garden; Mr Potteral from the Theatre Royal, Smock Alley; Mr and Mrs Freeman from the Theatre Royal, York and other respectable performers.

> He flatters himself that there never was such a company (in point of merit) yet seen in the North of Ireland, and he makes no doubt of their meeting with that candour and encouragement, that the town of Belfast are at all times ready and willing to show.

This was the press release for the coming season and followed his announcement that the theatre would reopen in early October 1786, and it did, with Mr Lewes starring in *Rule a Wife and Have a Wife*.

Back in 1785 he was proving his boast to provide the best for Belfast by engaging the two leading actresses of the day, sisters Mrs Sarah Siddons and Mrs Kemble, who performed in a run of several plays.

Sarah Siddons was at the time considered to be the greatest tragedy queen of the English stage, proving that she deserved the accolade by rounding off her visit with ten nights as Lady Macbeth.

On the Friday evening, 24 June, a benefit night for Mrs Kemble was held. While Mrs Siddons led in *Isabella*, she played second fiddle to her sister in the farce that followed, called *The Citizen*. It is known that in 1802 and 1803 her fee was forty guineas per night.

Atkins, whose theatre roots are now permanently in Belfast, must have been held in high regard by his stars, for these prominent actors and actresses returned time and time again. Down the line, watch out for both Mrs Siddons and Mr Lewes, just two of the returnees.

Atkins continued to promote, manage and find time to star. On Wednesday 5 January 1791 he once again took the lead in *Romeo and Juliet*. He remained in control until the theatre's final evening on 30 March 1793.

On the final evening a benefit for Mrs Richards was held. It was the Irish premiere of a new comedy entitled *Next Door Neighbours*, followed by Sheridan's *The Reign of Accomplishment*, and in a 'value for money' evening, a bizarrely named, yet apparently serious pantomime, *The Death of Captain Cook*.

Why, if Rosemary Lane was so successful, was it closing down? Simply because Atkins was on the move again. He probably received a better offer and couldn't resist the challenge of running a very large theatre.

There was a month's overlap as he went to his new home, The New Theatre in Arthur Square, and for that short period he was burning the candle at both ends, looking after the two properties.

It would be a long way down the road, and much theatre and music hall history would flow under the bridge, before the New Theatre site would be home to the Royal Cinema in 1916.

One point worth noting as Atkins does it all again, is the willingness of top performers to travel. Back then it was by a swaying, uncomfortable, stage coach and a none-too-pleasant sea voyage.

To date, a fair summing up of Michael Atkins' career would be 'when one door closes another one opens'. The New Theatre, which opened in 1793 and eventually became The Theatre Royal, was his fifth venue in an illustrious career.

It took a long time for the proverbial penny to drop, as far as I was concerned. This was in part due to the smokescreen created when each new theatre was built. No matter what, with the exception of Ann Street, they regularly reverted to using just 'Theatre' to describe themselves.

By simply not being sufficiently eagle-eyed, and ignoring the blatant increase in advertisements for 'theatre' in early 1790, I missed the obvious.

In the early days of my research, I had spotted that George Benn in *A History of the Town of Belfast from the Earliest Times to the Close of the Eighteenth Century* had written that in 1792, 'the Theatre in Arthur Street, lately renewed, has been levelled and been replaced in the same spot by a much larger structure, as a direct result of Atkins pledging that he will expend £2,000 in improving the theatre of the town.'

I could find no reference elsewhere. I saw what I felt were clues to its existence, but was constantly frustrated and misled by the advertisement. I had all but forgotten the issue, when glancing at Raymond Gillespie and Stephen A. Royle's *Belfast – Part 1 to 1840*, I found the missing link.

In it they wrote that 'the Theatre' opened to replace Rosemary Street, which until now I had taken to be the future Theatre Royal. Then they swept away all my misunderstandings, as clear and unambiguous references to the Belfast Theatre in Arthur Street West were made. And I now know why Atkins shut down Rosemary Lane and recognise the opportunity he saw to raise the money and expand.

I searched and searched but found no clearly identifiable advertisement for it, nor for its opening in 1790. Gillespie and Royle add that in 1791 the title was 'New Playhouse'. No luck there either. So its place in theatre history is that it provided a space for its very successful replacement, which saw Atkins in control.

Old Donegall Arms

The original Donegall Arms Hotel was often referred to as 'the New Inn', which was the name of the previous establishment on the site. It fronted Castle Place with a clear view up Cornmarket, past the Market House on the corner of High Street to its left.

THEATRE, BELFAST.

On WEDNESDAY next,

The COMEDY of
Much Ado About Nothing.

BEATRICE, by

Miſs BRUNTON.

With

High Life Below Stairs.

A Charity Sermon

Is to be preached on Sunday the 19th Instant, In the Old Meeting-houſe of Antrim, for the ſupport of the Sunday School in that town.

August 8th, 1787.

'Theatre, Belfast' here is referring to the Rosemary Lane venue. Friday 10 August 1787.

Today its location would be where the entrance to the Donegall Arcade is in Rosemary Street, opposite the Rosemary Street Non-Subscribing Presbyterian Church.

Thanks to its existence before 1752, it was well established early in the second half of the eighteenth century. Its official address being 11 Castle Place, it was the chief inn for at least a century, and was also the meeting place for various societies.

I have only found a few advertisements in the *Belfast Newsletter*. The one included below was the clearest to read and gives an insight into its programme and the fact that the theatre was 'at the back of the green'. It is almost certainly the 'Little Theatre', dated as being in existence from 1773-1778 by Gillespie and Royle. This ad appeared in the *Belfast Newsletter*, Friday 11 January 1788.

Mr Manuel will entertain the Company with that extraordinary Piece of Performance called ROSINGALL, of Warbling, Whistling and imitating the notes of various birds – 1st, the blackbird; 2nd, the rook; 3rd, the robin; 4th, the quail; 5th the nightingale; 6th, the peewitte; and 7th, the skylark – likewise whistling the notes and … the … Middle in a droll manner, etc.

For the clockwork, ombres chinoises and mechanical fireworks, for hand-bills – to begin at half-past after seven o'clock.

Pit 1s 7d half p, Gallery 1s 1d

The Theatre Royal

On Friday 22 February 1793 the *Belfast Newsletter* carried the following advertisement:

NEW THEATRE – ARTHUR STREET

We will be open on Monday next, 25 inst., with a favourite play and farce as will be expressed in the bills.

Tickets to be had of Mr Atkins, Arthur Street and Places in the Porch taken of Mr Mooney, Door-Keeper at Box Office everyday from 11 o'clock till 7.

It seems at this point that the intrepid Michael Atkins is involved in the birth of another theatre, and appears to have been involved in a takeover of some kind.

He was still there more than a decade later and in 1795 he was publicly acknowledged as 'a veteran manager of the theatre'. He certainly was this, for his career had begun in Belfast way back in the 1760s. His latest venture opened on the site of Lord Donegall's boathouse, at the corner of Arthur Street and Castle Lane.

Once again, his experience and expertise would be tested to the full, for this was Belfast's first large auditorium. It opened to the town's citizens with a seating capacity of approximately 1,100.

It was another first for the already impressive résumé of Atkins, as he initiated a venture that would see the Theatre Royal undergo a name change, several makeovers and a fire that would see it burn to the ground and be rebuilt in six months. It eventually closed on 10 March 1915. In its later years, Joseph F. Warden was in charge from about 1863 onwards.

Atkins, as I've already mentioned, was always looking to move onwards and upwards, especially if his present venture was perhaps on the slide or he was just losing interest. He obviously enjoyed a challenge, which is probably why he ended up raising the £2,000 referred to in the previous chapter and used it to resurrect the building on the Arthur Square site, demolishing the former Belfast Theatre in the process.

Atkins put his stamp on his new acquisition. In its early years it showed serious drama, with a liberal sprinkling of Shakespearean features. Mingled with these performances was a wide variety of charity benefit nights, comedies, a promotion of music hall, and in the years ahead there would also be ballet, Gilbert and Sullivan, opera, and at least one pure variety concert.

Before its closure in 1915, Paganini performed with his violin and Lily Langtry, Sarah Bernhardt and Mrs Patrick Campbell also took to the stage. A few years before the final curtain came down, citizens had a week in which to go along and see Anna Pavlova dance.

Even if the name of Atkins had not appeared in print, any self-respecting detective could have built a circumstantial case to prove it, for his favourite drama, and his favourite actors and actresses made an almost immediate appearance. Lee Lewes of Rosemary Lane fame was first on stage, and in 1802 Mrs Siddons swept into town, as Atkins continued his theme of serious drama interpreted by top stage stars.

Missing from the cast list for the first time was his own name, for after 1793 I could find no reference to him going onstage, not even in the early 1793 productions of *Romeo and Juliet*, *Richard the Third* or *Alexander the Great*.

Between the periods of control by Atkins and Warden there was constant change at the top, but before all of that, there was something still to be resolved. Myron Hamilton's 1783 appeal for funds kept Ann Street open, though I can find no identifiable advertisements after 1784.

Theatre Royal,
BELFAST.

SEASON TICKET,
Commencing Aug. 21, 1865.

Mr. *T. McClean*

No. 5   *Signed,*

DRESS CIRCLE.
NOTE.—*This Ticket is not available for Opera.*

Courtesy of the Belfast Central Library Theatre Collection.

George Benn did. He records a theatrical advertisement that read 'The Theatre in Ann Street must be enlarged and subscriptions are solicited for the purpose. It is proposed to make it ten feet wider and five feet higher'. There is no acknowledgement that this ever came about. It is at this stage that his book refers to the 1792 demolition of the existing theatre in Arthur Street, in order to make way for the replacement Ann Street theatre.

The opening of Arthur Street's newest venue comes right at the end of a period of great interest in the theatre, and the public who could afford to, attended in droves. There is always a choice of seating; a box, or a place in the pit, the stalls or the gallery.

Apart from special occasions when the price of a ticket might be a guinea (£1.10), it is hard to find advertisements detailing admission charges. However, for the sake of comparison, the theatre-goer at Ann Street or Mill Gate would have paid 5s 5d (27 ½ p) for a box, 3s 3d (16p) for the pit and 2s 2d (11p) for the gallery.

Atkins faced an early challenge, for in 1794 a floor collapsed, necessitating closure for emergency work to be carried out. It soon opened again. Michael Atkins' love affair with the theatre in his adopted Belfast continued until around 1806 when, for a few years, management passed to a Mr Bellamy.

Bellamy controlled its affairs successfully until 1809, before he sold to Mr Talbot. Talbot had theatrical and entrepreneurial ambitions and purchased not only this theatre, but theatres in Derry and Newry as well.

The new owner showed his commitment to the Arthur Street theatre, for after marrying, he settled into a house on the same street.

Michael Atkins, a man with an immense capacity for promoting theatre in his adopted town, simply disappeared off the radar after 1806. I would love to have heard of the final scene of his lengthy career.

The transition in management from Mr Bellamy to Mr Talbot was obviously a smooth one, and one well handled by a Mr Gordon, who had facilitated the arrangement. The new theatre impresario clearly thought so, for, in what appears to be Talbot's first public announcement of the changeover, he both praises and rewards Gordon, appointing him second-in-command at the theatre.

> From the satisfaction the public have expressed of Mr Gordon's grandeur as an acting manager, and abilities as a performer, Mr Talbot has been induced to engage him in both capacities.

Talbot continued with a wide-ranging programme, travelling to his other two acquisitions on a regular basis. His opening bill in Belfast on 27 January 1809 featured the tragedy *Popular* with the farce *Raising the Wind*.

As well as informing the public of his purchases in Newry and Derry and praising Mr Gordon, Talbot—in his speech—let them know that he had employed a company deserving their approbation, and he made the following remark:

> Mr Talbot begs leave to acquaint the Nobility and Gentry, Inhabitants of Belfast and the Vicinity.

Fires had been kept for some time in the theatre, and a stove and chimney were erected in the lobby. It was hoped this would lure the audiences in from outside.

Easter Monday, 20 April 1835, appears to be the date on which the next change in ownership took place; an actor who had been appearing regularly 'bought out' Talbot. In a very descriptive advertisement in the *Belfast Newsletter* of Wednesday 15 April, the actor listed his renovations, which were extensive. Mr Burroughs was certainly putting his best foot forward.

It is worth noting just a few of the main changes. The site was enlarged and extended; the auditorium entirely repaired, embellished and remodelled; the circle and boxes ornamented with striking pictorial representations; a gas chandelier and a new drop curtain were both installed.

In addition, he fitted in private boxes, had the stock scenery repainted, strengthened his company, and improved the wardrobe and stage-support system.

His shows varied greatly and there was a distinct feel of music hall in the air at times. On Monday 26 October 1835, a 'Grand Masquerade' was held, combining a great variety of entertainment. The stage was enlarged, and for those planning to attend, costumes could be got at the theatre.

Many of his evenings turned out to be the forerunners of the cine-variety theatres that would appear once the silent movie era arrived. For those audiences, his mix and match was drama and variety, and was his attempt to compete with the premises being given over to various kinds of music hall performances.

A good example is that of Friday evening, 3 November 1837. Sheridan's *The Rivals* was the main feature, backed by a troupe of Bedouin Arabs and popular songs by Miss Carr. For four nights only, the celebrated comedian Mr Power entertained audiences, from Monday 15 to Thursday 18, 1839. Burrough's stay lasted until the end of 1840.

Next in the catalogue of those in charge is Mr Thorbourne. Like all those before him, he was an actor and regularly appeared on stage. On Monday 25 January 1841 he took the helm. 'Under the immediate management or Mr Thorbourne', proclaims his first advertisement, and he was determined to raise standards.

Belfast Newsletter, Wednesday 11 April 1835.

It is respectfully suggested that visitors to Dress Boxes, especially at this season of the year,
should avail themselves of the custom now observed by the Patrons of the Theatre Royal in
London, namely to occupy their place in Dress suited to their own convenience and the season.

His wish was that everyone should feel at home, no matter what area they sat in. To encourage
this, he had an extra stove fitted, and informed citizens that 'good fires will be kept in all parts
of the house'.

Wherever they chose to sit on opening night, they would have seen him act in *The Wife – A
Tale of Mantua*, filling the role of Julien St Pierre. The following Monday he trod the boards in
King Henry the Fourth and continued until his sell-out to one Mr Cunningham in 1843, who
labelled himself 'acting manager' and was sole lessee until he passed the managerial-relay baton
to Mr Charles Poole.

This was obviously an amicable arrangement, as the notice for 7 January 1853 proves, stating
that 'The Theatre Royal is now open every evening under the management of Mr Charles Poole'.
In November of that year all three appeared in *Macbeth*, with Charles as the third witch.

The name was changed to the Theatre Royal, presumably as a response to and in honour of the visit to Belfast by Queen Victoria on 11 August 1849. The last use of the name 'Theatre—Arthur Street' was on Saturday 26 April 1852, with Theatre Royal appearing in an advertisement on Monday 28.

Mr Cooke's time in command ended in the late 1850s, when Joseph F. Warden bought the building and became proprietor, holding his opening night on 26 January 1863. The grand opening evening featured Professor Anderson's new entertainment, *Prestidigitation*, with all effects produced (solely) by manual skill. Other variety occasions followed, but one instantly recognisable name is Paganini, who made his appearance in the week of 5 November 1866. On Monday 12 November, for one night only, he appeared at the Ulster Hall (opened in 1862).

In March 1871 the Old Theatre Royal was demolished by Warden and rebuilt within six months, opening for business on 25 September 1871, with a five-act comedy aptly named *Time Works Wonders*. Warden was the sole proprietor and manager, and he was determined that his new design would attract more well-to-do audiences.

The new building rose to 80 feet, with a frontage of 107 feet, stretching along Arthur Square and down Castle Lane. Its four-storey arcaded façade was made of brick, with no expense spared inside or out. When the doors opened in Arthur Square, and round the corner in Castle Lane, 2,200 people flocked in. This was twice the capacity of the former theatre.

Prices ranged from *6d* (2 ½ p) for the gallery to *30s* (£1.50) or *40s* (£2) for private boxes. Special trains ran on the Holywood and Bangor Railway, leaving at 11.15 p.m. after the performances.

Warden must have been unhappy with its décor, for at the end of the first season he ordered a complete redecoration.

A *Belfast Morning News* journalist almost ran out of superlatives when describing the overall new look. It must have been magnificent. 'It has been transformed into a gorgeous and commodious temple … pillars supporting the proscenium are decorated with Pompeian and Greek ornaments … walls of the lower boxes are hung with mirrors … a handsome gas bracket between each pair of boxes … a ceiling with handsome Italian ornaments … scenes from *Romeo and Juliet*; of Hamlet's ghost; of Macbeth's witches, etc., adorn the panels'.

All this and much more was overseen by James Dobson from Dublin, whose firm was responsible for the decoration of the Dublin Gaiety Theatre.

Ten years later Warden had to do it again when, at around 8 a.m. on Wednesday 8 June 1881, his theatre was reduced to four bare walls, some tottering pillars, and a few blackened beams following a devastating fire. This was a fate that had befallen the Alhambra eight years earlier and hundreds more in the UK around this period.

Perhaps it was a mixed blessing, for a friend of Warden's was heard to remark, 'Well, I'm sorry for Mr Warden's sake', as he watched the flames take their last lick of 'the dear, dirty house, but I'm exceedingly glad to see the end of many scenes (décor) I detested.' A benefit was held in the Alhambra for its actors. It was packed out with almost no standing room available. On 14 June in the Working Men's Institute, a benefit took place for the band whose instruments had been destroyed.

Despite all the wear and tear, the phoenix was about to rise from the ashes.

Undaunted by the catastrophe of March 1881, Warden immediately commissioned 'a model theatre'. With a speed that would have been unbelievable in that day and age, his new venture opened its doors on 22 December 1881, and the Theatre Royal was back.

It was, according to its own publicity, 'one of the most elegant, commodious and substantial structures in the Three Kingdoms'. World-renowned tragedian Barry Sullivan left his partial retirement to appear for the opening of the new theatre, and Mr Warden addressed the audience

THIS EVENING.

THE BURNING OF THE THEATRE ROYAL.

WORKING MEN'S INSTITUTE.

GRAND VOCAL AND INSTRUMENTAL
CONCERT,

On TUESDAY EVENING, June 14th,

FOR THE BENEFIT

OF THE

BAND OF THE THEATRE ROYAL, BELFAST,

Who had their Instruments destroyed
by the Fire.

Madame Schroeder, Miss S. E. Moore, Mr. T. Picton, Mr. W. J. Moore, Mr. T. Nerney, Herr Werner, and a number of Gentlemen have kindly given their services.

Tickets—Reserved Seats, 3s ; Second Seats, 2s ; Back Seats, 1s. Concert to commence at Eight o'clock.
6056

Belfast Telegraph, Tuesday 14 June 1881.

after the opening event. Lord Lynton's famous *Comedy of Money* was shown that Thursday evening, while Barry Sullivan, 'the Cardinal', appeared in *Richelien* on Friday 23.

In a newspaper article entitled *Before and Behind the Footlights*, the theatre is described as being 'tastefully finished in the modern style with elaborate carvings, pleasant walls, subdued upholstery and overall … extremely handsome'.

However, Warden's resident artists, Bellair and O'Farrell, were criticised elsewhere. Stung by this, he engaged a Mr Swift, described as 'a clever artist', to upgrade his new scenery.

'Arthur Square' was a success, prompting Warden to think of diversifying. He acted by building the Grand Opera House in 1895. It was a venture that did not quite work out, mainly due to a failure to identify the type of audience it might attract. His son Fred made the decision to rename the Opera House, 'The Palace of Varieties', and the smaller theatre turned exclusively to drama. The decision was met with a highly critical media storm.

Large-scale shows had been costly to bring to the house, and the Opera House's cheaper seats were almost always full. The dearer ones that needed to sell out rarely did. Warden tried reducing the Royal's prices, attempting to infer that quality lay elsewhere. It failed as a strategy. The patrons of both were left in a quandary and audiences in the two projects fluctuated wildly.

The truth was that even before the Grand Opera House turned 'music hall', audiences were flocking to the nearby venues of the Empire, the Alhambra, the Olympia Palace and the Star. The Royal Hippodrome (1907) in turn also added to the decline of the Theatre Royal, and soon the silent movies would come along.

The Theatre Royal bowed to the inevitable on 10 March 1915, leaving memories of past glories; among them were such performances as the Carl Rosa Opera and the best of Gilbert and Sullivan, by Richard D'Oyle Carte's company.

Way back on 6 August 1888, Joseph Warden was proud to boast—and rightly so—that, for the first time in Ireland, his audience would be protected by a fireproof curtain.

Many of the great names from the British stage had come to this theatre. Lily Langtry (1852–1929), whose private life filled the gossip columns of the day, was there several times. After her week beginning 23 November 1885, one reviewer stated 'In spite of her personal lifestyle and setting it aside … surrounded by a strong cast, she was undoubtedly outstanding'. The Langtry family led Belfast's shipping industry, no doubt one reason for her popularity amongst the citizens. Two other great actresses, Madam Sarah Bernhardt and Mrs Patrick Campbell, appeared together and ended their week of performances in the middle of July 1905.

As the final years rolled by, the 'Dancing Revelation of the Age', Anna Pavlova, arrived directly from the Imperial Opera House, St Petersburg, and Royal Opera House, Covent Garden, with the company of the Imperial Russian Ballet. They appeared every night for the week of 29 January 1912.

When the *Belfast Telegraph* published the venue's final press release, the 'home' of legitimate theatre for so many years must have felt it like a stab in the back. The release stated, 'The progress and popularity of the cinematograph have induced Messrs Warden to embark on a fresh venture and have resolved to raze the Theatre Royal to the ground and in its place a stately, commodious picture house.' The building was given a rousing send-off by artists from the Alhambra, Hippodrome and Empire, among others. It was an occasion when 'standing room was at a premium'.

The Royal Cinema opened on 16 December 1916 with *The Misleading Lady*, but was demolished in 1961. On a final note, this was the same theatre that opened its doors back on Thursday 23 December 1841, in order to allow the owner of the neighbouring Shakespeare Hotel to promote his premises, when launching itself as a music hall. I am fairly sure that the first film was shown there on 17 February 1902, with matinees on Wednesdays and Saturdays. Promotions ran for quite a while.

NOTE Each adult paying for admission will have the privilege of bringing two children
– free of charge to all parts (except gallery one child free).
BELFAST DAY BY DAY
Look out for yourself in Edison's Pictures.
Prices of admission – 2s, 1s, 6d.

TO-DAY, at 2.　　　　TO-NIGHT, at 7-50.

THEATRE ROYAL.

TO-NIGHT, at 7-30, and during the week.
MATINEES TO-DAY (WEDNESDAY),
January 31, and FRIDAY NEXT,
February 2, at 2-0 p.m.
THE EVENT OF THE CENTURY.
DANIEL MAYER presents

ANNA PAVLOVA,

The DANCING REVELATION of the AGE!
Direct from her Triumph at the Imperial
Opera House, St. Petersburg; Royal Opera,
Covent Garden, London; Palace Theatre, London, and

MONS. NOVIKOFF,

with Members of the Imperial Russian Ballet,
including Mons. CHIRIAIEFF, Madame BOUT-
KOVSKA, and Madame CHARPENTIER.
Circle and Stalls, 6s, can be reserved. Upper
Circle and Pit, 3s. Gallery, 1s. Box Office
daily, 10 to 5. Telephone 1142.

Belfast Newsletter, 29 January–3 February 1912.

THEATRE ROYAL.

TO-MORROW (WEDNESDAY), at 7.30.

GRAND COMPLIMENTARY BENEFIT

TO STAFF OF THEATRE ROYAL.

MONSTRE PROGRAMME.

SEE SPECIAL BILLS.

Prices, 6d to 2s. Seats can now be booked.

Belfast Newsletter, Friday 20 August 1852.

Above left: Closing adverts. *Belfast Newsletter,* 11 April 1891.

Above right: The Star Music Hall closed for renovation, after which its reopening was announced in the *Belfast Newsletter* on 8 August 1893.

St George's Hall

St George's Hall is still in existence today. It can be found at the foot of Bridge Street, across the road in High Street. The architecture stands out and is quite striking, but sadly the building is no longer in use. It was entered at first-floor level after ascending a staircase between business premises. Perhaps it was named after St George's Parish Church, which was built in 1816 and is located near St George's Hall. The hall was built in either 1881 or 1882, though I could not find an exact date. The first advertisement I came across, dated 24 October, gave its opening date as Monday 30 October 1882.

St George's gave itself over to a variety of uses and was, in its way, unique. It was designed as a large public hall with a seating capacity in excess of 1,205. It became, in turn, a variety hall, a café, a music hall, and a cinema. I personally remember it as a boxing arena.

Then on Monday 30 October, the *Belfast Newsletter* carried an interesting advert (see page 106). Could this be where the saying 'a laugh a minute' arose?

The hall certainly came highly recommended, aided by the low admission costs of two shillings (10p), 1 shilling (5p) and sixpence (2 ½ p).

The music hall/variety nature of the shows lasted for just over a decade, with a blockbuster appearing every so often, such as *Uncle Tom's Cabin* which opened on Monday 16 October 1893, with a midday performance for schools on Saturdays.

Continuing my search on into 1894, I found there was suddenly no St George's Hall. Apparently it closed down early in the New Year, but a September advert announced it as a restaurant, complete with all the latest attractions to tempt the discerning public. As the advertisement, dated Tuesday 18 September 1894, states, 'This is the entire St George's Hall remodelled'.

In time the popularity of the large, seemingly upmarket café/restaurant waned and it resumed its former role. It is hard to know why it was not successful, as it was centrally located and even had a smoking gallery for the men and a room for the ladies. It must simply have been a casualty of changing times.

Until 1908 St George's Hall stuck with the variety theme, staging individual artists, shows and pantomimes. After this, it moved with the times and became a cinema, eventually closing in 1916.

There is little to be said about the Great George's Street Music Hall, or its exact location. For having chanced upon its advertisements, few and far between as they were, a meticulous search of Belfast street directories proved fruitless.

It operated in the 1880s and opened on Mondays, Thursdays and Saturdays. Advertisements always seemed to refer to 'amateur selections' and it seems this venue was often the training ground for local talent.

The advertisements on the following page are typical of the few I found.

The Ulster Hall

It is difficult to imagine that at one time the Ulster Hall was considered a music hall. Not only that, but it was also the largest in the British Isles, with a capacity of 3,500.

Since its opening on Monday 12 May 1862 it played a vital role in the Belfast entertainment scene. It was home to a magnificent Mulholland Organ and it played host to everything from individual acts to orchestral concerts, food fests to mass rallies, wrestling and boxing matches to schools, concert services, and everything in between.

ST. GEORGE'S HALL, HIGH STREET

Mr. GEO. LINGARD, sole proprietor and manager.
GRAND OPENING NIGHT,
MONDAY, October 30th, of
Professor S. S. and CLARA BALDWIN (late of St. James's Hall, London), in their world-renowned entertainment of SPIRITUALISM EXPOSED. For future announcements see daily papers and posters. 18179

ST. GEORGE'S HALL,
HIGH STREET.

Mr. GEO. LINGARD, sole proprietor and manager.
TO-NIGHT, TO-NIGHT, TO-NIGHT,
And every Evening during the Week,
THE LATEST AMERICAN AND ENGLISH SENSATION, from St. James's Great Hall, Regent Street, London,

PROF. S. S. & CLARA BALDWIN,
SPIRIT EXPOSERS AND THOUGHT READERS,

In the Funniest Entertainment ever given—150 Laughs in 150 Minutes. You can actually see and recognise dead friends at Mrs. Baldwin's
SPIRIT BRIDE RECEPTION.
SPIRITUALISM OUTDONE AND EXPOSED, THOUGHT READING, CLAIRVOYANCY.

Endorsed by over 1,000 Clergymen, Nobility, Professors, and the Literati generally. See Bills.

Admission—2s, 1s, and 6d, a few Choice Reserved Seats at 2s 6d. Doors open at 7·15, commence at 8. Carriages may be ordered for 10 15.

Box Office for Reserved Seats at Messrs. HART & CHURCHILL's, Castle Place. 18179

Above: Opening night, *Belfast Newsletter,* 30 October 1882.

Left: Belfast Newsletter, Monday 30 October 1882.

OPENING NOTICE.

ST. GEORGE'S CAFE RESTAURANT.

THIS SPLENDID CAFE

IS NOW OPEN.

SPACIOUS DINING-ROOM (40ft. High).

LADIES' ROOM,

PRIVATE ROOMS,

EXCELLENT SMOKING GALLERY.

THIS IS THE ENTIRE ST. GEORGE'S HALL REMODELLED.

AND CONVERTED INTO A CAFE, AND HAS BEEN IN THE HANDS OF THE BUILDER AND DECORATOR FOR THAT PURPOSE SINCE FEBRUARY LAST.

HIGH STREET (Opposite Bridge Street).

POPULAR TARIFF.

Belfast Telegraph, Tuesday 18 September 1894.

Harry Lauder (Mander & Mitchenson, 1965).

HIPPODROME AND CIRCUS
Under the distinguished patronage of the
Lord Mayor (Sir Daniel Daow)
A change of programme will be introduced weekly

The promise of weekly programme changes was kept, and while the opening events were almost pure circus, over the years the emphasis shifted to include music hall acts. However, come Christmas and Easter there was always a return to circus acts with a wide range of performers, from aerial gymnasts to Little Valdo, 'the Earth's funniest clown'. The New Imperial Hippodrome and Circus was in Chichester Street and, while no exact address is given, it is most likely that it was at the junction with Victoria Street, where the Equestrian Arena stood. This is supported by the fact that there seemed to be a resident group of performing horses.

It became known as the Grand Hippodrome and was in full flow by the end of 1906, though I lost track of it in 1907. At no time did I see advertisements for any appearances by music hall star performers.

Belfast folk loved a good circus, and in the nineteenth century they were spoilt for choice. So frequent were the visits by different circuses that it seems safe to say that they were fuelling an addiction!

They ran alongside entertainment on offer in the theatre or music halls, while talks and concerts, art displays, magic shows and regattas, held for one purpose or another, were reasons to 'go out and enjoy'.

Almost week after week a circus arrived to feed the insatiable demand. To give an idea of their place in the overall scheme of things, I have selected a few to focus on.

Belfast circus had its roots in open spaces on the fringes of the town. One venue in particular was close to the site of our prestigious Waterfront Hall, that of Batty's Circus.

Batty's Circus eventually found a permanent home in Chichester Street, housing an audience well in excess of a thousand. It was there, on 18 January 1841, that Daniel O'Connell spoke. Early advertisements list it as the 'Circus Royal Belfast' and the site was called the 'National Olympic Arena'. I have had to assume that these are one and the same as the details match up.

As an aside, it is said that the Olympic Arena once had to apologise to its prospective audiences in January 1840, and announce that 'with deep regret, due to the cage to hold lions, tigers and leopards, etc., having failed to arrive ...' there would be a curtailed programme.

Batty's later appears at one of the other central sites in the mid 1840s. This, at 12 Wellington Place on the corner of Upper Queen Street, was the only one I could fix at a permanent location until 1852.

There was another regular spot in Howard Street, but a *Belfast Street Directory* search failed to pinpoint it. However, there were many unregistered occupancies and, undoubtedly, the circus found a home in one.

Everyone who visits Belfast will almost certainly have gazed at the spot on the corner of Great Victoria Street and Glengall Street. Before the Grand Opera House and prior to the Olympia Palace, it was the spot where the circus had found a home. Hence the use of 'cirque' in the present title high up on the façade.

The Olympia Palace (formerly Ginnett's Circus) and the street directories provide the proof, and several writers have stated that the Grand Opera House was built on the site of a circus.

Ginnett's family circus was always called 'Ginnett's Circus Hippodrome and Olympia', worth a mention for the name of 'Olympia Palace' and of course 'The Royal Hippodrome'.

Ginnett's, like Batty's, had a permanent home, which from 1882 held 2,000 people, before being remodelled as 'the Olympia Palace' at No. 5 Glengall Place.

Number 5 played host to many circuses over the years, but Ginnett's was by far the most frequent tenant. Cooke's was another, as was Harmston. The latter, when appearing at the start of January 1883, billed itself as 'The Equestrian Palace of Amusements, Recreation, Cleanliness and Comfort'. In spite of Ginnett's strong association with the address, it is the Harmiston circus that must take the credit for erecting the structure in Glengall Place.

In the *Belfast Evening Telegraph* (Monday 13 November 1882), the public's attention was drawn to the fact that Harmston's Grand Continental Circus would open for a short season on Saturday 18 November, with a most talented troupe of male and female equestrians, gymnasts, acrobats, athletes and clowns, and a highly trained team of horses and ponies and other performing animals.

The 'new structure' was described in detail on Saturday 11: the main entrance was in Glengall Place, and the splendid building featured a promenade running almost entirely around it. The spacious vestibule had a couple of handsome staircases opening onto the promenade and, wherever you sat, the view was unobstructed. The exits were such that a building holding around 2,000 would, in an emergency, be emptied in the space of two or three minutes. Health and safety was at a standard of excellence. Remember, Harmiston knew that both the Royal Alhambra and the Theatre Royal burnt down in 1873 and 1881 respectively.

Ginnett's was still in family hands after more than two hundred years on the road but was then threatened by government legislation. Apparently, the government had issued earlier assurances that when new legislation was introduced requiring a duty of £500 per site to be paid for setting up a performance, circuses would be excluded. However, this proved to be false and Ginnett's owners' response was to say that as the circus was itinerant by nature, such a levy every time they moved could force closure.

One of the last circuses to visit 12 Wellington Place was Pablo Fanque's Royal Circus in the year 1851 'exhibiting the unrivalled Equestrian and Gymnastic Corps'. Soon after this, the action moved to a location in Howard Street, where among those appearing towards the end of February 1855 was an American circus under the management of Mr Richard Bell. The 1850s was a popular decade for circuses, and there were many in existence.

November 1857 found 'Bell's Monster Circus' in Victoria Street but, frustratingly, I could not find the exact location. It was not a once-off location, for others followed. The emphasis at Bell's was on equestrian events, although mention is made of the inclusion of clowns and various troupes. In September 1860 Hengler's 'Equestrian Palace' was billed, and its performances appear to be more in line with our idea of a circus than any of its rivals.

I found references to circus performances in Victoria Street until well into the second half of the 1860s. In April 1866 Quaglieni's New Cirque captivated the crowds.

Away from circus life, menageries—some travelling, some permanent—attracted visitors. Not quite a circus, not quite a zoo, they gave the public a 'wildlife experience'. They were a huge attraction in the town.

One of the largest arrived in Victoria Street in February 1855, when Mander's Royal Menagerie brought what was described as a 'truly surprising collection of wild beasts, birds and reptiles'.

I have referred only to the nineteenth century, but in my reading I found references, which I did not pursue, to circuses in the late eighteenth century. From then until the final years, when the Royal Hippodrome held its 'Christmas Circus', there is a clear trail to be followed.

The Great Outdoors

While the transition from the rowdy indoor scene in the pubs and saloons to the more upmarket variety music halls was underway, there was a parallel open-air transformation taking place. The outdoor entertainment was naturally governed by the weather and accordingly ran from Easter through the summer.

Eventually it would move to the Harland and Wolff side of Belfast Lough, but the outdoor tradition began on the opposite side, and developed on the slopes of the Cave Hill, easily accessible from the town.

The Cave Hill was a Mecca for all on Easter Monday, and to a lesser extent on other occasions. This was pure open-air entertainment—sideshows with more than enough drink to wash the food down. The revelry on the slopes offended church representatives, who were scandalised by the 'unseemly' behaviour of those having a good time. Vociferous protests followed the 'over-indulgence'.

Perhaps respectability won out, as attendance began to dwindle and the action transferred to Dargan's Island, which in turn became Queen's Island.

Unlike the Cave Hill, this venue in its early stages was a one-day wonder. Later, other events occurred that increased its popularity, such as fêtes. The Cave Hill's demise was hastened by the emergence of attractive alternatives. The age of the railways was at hand and escape from the town was possible. Thoroughfares were better, and a cruise down the lough on a Bangor Steamer was a highlight. Initially, this trip was an adventure, but as the face of entertainment and popular amusement changed in the late 1840s and early 1850s, it became the norm.

At Easter, a ferry enabled you to visit the island for a 1d fare. The large patch of reclaimed land, added to by the dredging from the new Victoria Channel, was 'Funland' for the visitors, a huge pleasure park, and set out as such.

It was a wonderland for adults and children alike and held Belfast's first zoo, with a huge conservatory and a menagerie featuring a pheasant, racoon, monkey and a golden eagle.

As the forerunner of amusement arcades, Funland didn't disappoint. The earliest version held what are now treasured museum pieces, among them some of the very first mechanical toys including peep-shows, but not of the titillating variety. These featured battles of historical importance and other historical scenes. Many were gruesome, such as the hangman and his gallows, the executioner beheading Charles II, even a pupil being caned.

A huge barrel organ entertained and sideshows abounded. Stalls sold food and drink, including poteen, with musicians playing until the last visitor left.

There was a great deal of spontaneity but it was, after all, about profit, and so it was much more tightly structured and better organised than amusements in the days of Cave Hill. It is said that the lessee took his money to the bank in the sacks used for the sack races!

The transition from Dargan to Queen's Island was simply a name-change and the pleasure-garden tradition continued into the middle of the 1870s. From the 1840s the island had been the playground of the inner-city poor. It disappeared almost overnight.

Donegall Quay and the aptly named Long Strand were places where the residents of Newtownard's Road came to relax, but in the end they had to sacrifice their recreational area for the newly expanded shipyard, which in the end served their area well, providing employment and increasing prosperity.

In spite of the continuing attractions at Queen's Island, Easter Monday went upmarket in the 1850s, moving location to the Royal Botanical Gardens. It remained a popular day for all the city's citizens. However, the focus was now on the gardens, where there were going to be concerts, garden fêtes, fireworks, and re-enactments of famous battles. All of these events made it 'the place to be seen'.

Today it is hard to envisage the Botanic Gardens stretching along the River Lagan, past the present Lyric Theatre and up to the roundabout at the junction of Stranmills Road. The first step was taken in 1827, when the decision to acquire land was made by the Belfast Palm and Horticultural Society, an area of fourteen acres in total.

A site was acquired in 1829, stretching from the present Queen's University building, through where the Palm House is, and on across the central space to the River Lagan. Admission from its earlier days until 1895 was by membership, and meetings of proprietors, and AGMs of shareholders and others, were held at such venues as the library, White Linen Hall, or the ballroom of the Commercial Buildings in Waring Street.

The Palm House opened in 1852 but not before a bazaar was held for the Royal Botanical Gardens in the New Corn Exchange, on Friday 13 and Saturday 14 February.

In aid of the funds for completing the conservatory in the Royal Botanical Gardens at which will be exhibited great attractions Electrical Telegraph, etc., with the stalls well and tastefully furnished, under the inspection, management and labour of the Ladies of Belfast and neighbourhood.

The Belfast Corporation bought the land and the gardens became free to all in 1895, and in 1902 the unique tropical ravine was added.

It is worth having a quick look at events at Queen's Island and in the Botanic Gardens. Events on Dargan Island, however, were something of a disappointment for me, as I just couldn't find an advertisement.

On Saturday 26 July 1851, Queen's Island was illuminated by a 'magnificent display of fireworks'. There was a portrait of 'Her Majesty, composed of better than five thousand jets of light'. A band performed to round off the formalities.

Access was by a pontoon bridge, illuminated by Chinese lanterns and the lights from the boats that arrived from Albert Quay and Prince's Dock. Admission, including the ferry, was one shilling; for the working class it was sixpence.

On Friday 16 August 1861, 7,000 spectators watched the 'Hero of Niagara' and 'King of the Tightrope'—the renowned Blondin performing a 500-foot wire act, 100 feet high. The show started in sunshine but finished in heavy showers, scattering the Botanical Gardens' crowd.

There were many fêtes and bazaars, held for a variety of reasons. One, for example, was organised by the Ladies' Committee to raise funds for the Botanic Conservatory. Public transport was improved for these events—as an advertisement stated, 'All the railway companies will run special trams to leave Belfast at ten o'clock'. That was on Friday 5 September 1851, to follow a fête and a splendid display of fireworks. In the 1850s the Victoria Fête and Bazaar was held in the Victoria Buildings, Queen's Island, and each year one was held to mark the anniversary of Queen Victoria's visit to Belfast in August 1849.

Musical contributions were common at these events, quite often from the army regiments stationed here. For example, on Easter Monday 24 March 1894, the band of the 51st King's Own

Belfast Newsletter,
2 June 1879.

Yorkshire Light Infantry appeared to mark the occasion of Captain Ortin's balloon ascent at 4.30 p.m.

On Easter Monday, 3 April 1893, the 1st Lancashire Fusiliers performed with the band of the 2nd Battalion Devonshire Regiment; Mlle Nana balanced on her head on a rope, while 'Cavier', the only boxing bear in the world, put on his gloves in a man versus bear fight. Captain Orton (again) took to the sky in his balloon.

In the last fête of the season in 1886, the splendid band of the Black Watch warmed up proceedings on Friday 17 September. They came up from the Curragh and were joined by the Senior Dragon Guards from Dundalk. The evening was brilliantly illuminated with 20,000 crystal lamps, and land- and water-based fireworks that illustrated a famous sea battle.

A grand pyrotechnic display took place on Whit Monday, 2 June 1879. The highlights were 'A Camera Obscura', appearing for the first time at a small additional charge, and a series of interesting experiments using dynamite fired by time fuses.

Finally, my favourite Botanic advertisement was for Monday 9 August 1852. With the new Palm House just ready, it must have provided a marvellous backdrop. There was a midday and

115

VICTORIA FETE AND BAZAAR.

Third Anniversary of her Majesty's Visit
to Belfast.

Under the distinguished Patronage of his Excellency
THE EARL OF EGLINTON,
Lord Lieutenant of Ireland.
VICE-PATRONS:
The Marquis of LONDONDERRY.
The Earl of BELFAST.
Lord DUFFERIN AND CLANDEBOYE.
The Lord Bishop of DOWN, CONNOR, and
DROMORE.
The Right Rev. Dr. DENVIR.

THE LADIES' COMMITTEE BEG TO
announce to the Nobility, Gentry, and Public of
Belfast and its Vicinity that

THE FANCY BAZAAR

will be Opened, in the VICTORIA BUILDING,
QUEEN'S ISLAND,

On FRIDAY, THE 20TH OF AUGUST,

at ELEVEN o'clock, Forenoon, the Building being
decorated with Flags, Banners, &c.

There will be a most extensive and varied assort-
ment of Work for Sale, comprising a variety of novel
and beautiful articles, amongst which will be found ex-
quisite specimens of FLOWERS, FRUIT, &c., in
WAX MODELLING; EMBROIDERY, of every description; FANCY-WORKED CUSHIONS; CHAIR-
COVERS; &c., &c.

A HANDSOME DRAWING-ROOM SCREEN,
which was Balloted for last year, and having been won
by one of the Committee, was re-presented by him for
this year's Bazaar, will again be Balloted for. It con-
tains several hundred of the best prints, and has been
valued at £40.

Tickets—2s. 6d, each.

THE POST-OFFICE

will be presided over by a number of youthful Post-
mistresses; and there will also be

A FAIRY FORTUNE TELLER.

THE LARGE AND ELEGANT FOUNTAIN,

erected last year, by Sig. Nannetti, and which has since
been much improved, will be in full play.

THE REFRESHMENT TABLES

will be most liberally supplied, at reasonable prices,
and will be presided over by Ladies of the Committee.

THE BRIDGE,

(FROM QUEEN'S QUAY TO THE ISLAND),

has been constructed similarly to that which, last year,
gave such universal satisfaction.

Fruit and Flowers requested from Ladies in the
Country, to be sent to the Industrial School, Frederick
Street, and any further Contributions of Work will be
received by

MISS MALCOLM,
Hon. Secretary Ladies' Committee,

Belfast Newsletter, Friday 20 August 1852.

evening performance, featuring a 'Powerful and Talented Troupe of British, French, Hungarian, German and American Equestrians'.

The event featured Arabian ponies, steeds of 'Tartar' breed, infant prodigies—really, you would need to read the full advertisement. Carriages were to 'be in attendance for day performance at half past four; Evening performance at half past nine o'clock precisely'.

Today, food fêtes, opera in the gardens and concerts continue in the tradition established around a century and a half ago.

Theatre-land Walkabout

While there are few traces of Belfast's old 'theatre-land' left in today's city, a stroll through the city streets will bring to life the days when theatre-going was a popular pastime. For the purpose of this 'tour', all venues will be regarded as being in existence at the same time in the present day.

What better point to commence the walkabout than at the doorstep of the magnificent Grand Opera House in Great Victoria Street and then walk on past its new frontage, where the Royal Hippodrome had stood. Previously on the Grand Opera House site were Ginnett's Circus and the Olympia Palace.

Passing the Hippodrome, we come to Grosvenor Road. A left turn here along the Hippodrome brings us to the Alexandra Theatre, aka the Palladium, aka the Colosseum, on the corner of Sandy Row.

Returning to the Hippodrome, we head down to the statue standing in front of the Royal Belfast Academical Institution. From here we cross into Wellington Place and go left into Queen's Street, walking down to Castle Street before going left at the junction. Three doors up stands the Mill Gate Theatre. Cross to the other side of the road and walk out of town to a busy intersection, where a right turn leads to Smithfield.

In Smithfield Square are the Royal Hibernian, the National and McCormick Theatres. Walk on to the next corner and pause there for a minute. Directly across Upper North Street, the very last building is the Gaiety, renamed the Star Bingo Hall.

Now look left, up the Shankill Road, for this is Peter's Hill. Just at the top of the rise the Lodge Road branches off to the right, and along it you will find the Lodge Theatre.

Wander down towards Royal Avenue and cross straight over to Lower North Street. Almost immediately, you will find Church Street leading directly to St Anne's Parish Church, today St Anne's Cathedral. Fifty yards onwards is William Street. Close to its corners are the Star Music Hall/the Office and the Star Bar.

Opposite them is the mouth of Long Lane, which moves to the right in an L-shaped fashion. We pass the Robert Burns Tavern Music Hall and go back to North Street. Continue a very short distance to Garfield Street and the Deer's Head Imbibing Emporium on the corner. Although the Royal Alhambra, just opposite the Deer's Head, has its own bar, many patrons crowd into the alternative across the street.

One hundred yards further on is the junction at the Four Corners, but the chance to see Oddfellows Hall, the notorious 'singing saloon', means a glance up the arcade leading to Donegall Street.

When the foot of North Street is reached, the spaciousness of Bridge Street is apparent and, looking down it, the striking architecture of St George's Hall is equally obvious. To the right is Rosemary Street, but looking in the opposite direction towards Waring Street, the Commercial Buildings on the Bridge Street corner can be seen. A few yards beyond them is the Thatched House Tavern.

Separating North Street and Donegall Street is the magnificent Exchange/Assembly Rooms Building, but before having the chance to gaze back up at them from the St George's Hall location, a detour along Rosemary Lane is a must. Go as far as Rosemary Street Presbyterian Church, where members of the congregation are watching Michael Atkins building his Rosemary Lane Play House.

Cornmarket is next, so walk along the Donegall Arcade which leads to Castle Place. Remember that behind its walls, to the right, is the Play House. As the exit is reached, the Donegall Arms Hotel and its Little Theatre complete its length. Imagine that standing outside are several stage coaches.

Another wide street leads to the open space at the heart of Cornmarket. On the left-hand corner, facing us, is the Market House and slipping up the dark, narrow lane on the right, the Plough Hotel and its Harmonie Saloon can be found on the left-hand corner of Castle Lane. A few steps down towards the Cornmarket is another 'singing saloon', but now known as the Shakespeare Music Hall.

This is the corner of Castle Lane and Arthur Street, around which curls the Theatre/Theatre Royal. Walk up Arthur Street, cross Chichester Street and there, in Music Hall Lane, sits the May Street Music Hall.

Back in Cornmarket, there are a few options. In the right-hand corner, the opening leads off to 16-18 Victoria Square, where, at various dates, the Imperial, the Colosseum, the Buffalo, the Bijou Empire and the Empire Theatre of Varieties had been in existence.

Directly across from here is Ann Street, and at No. 21 the Star Saloon and Music Hall, also called the Alhambra, faces the Pottinger entry. Walk along the street past the Morning Star and emerge in High Street to gaze directly at the Exchange, up at the Four Corners.

Look right for the Albert Clock and head towards it, passing St George's Church, near which is found the Sir Moses Cellars. Weigh House Lane is also here, where the Vaults are located. Also in this area is the Ann Street Theatre (the exact location unknown), and the Great George's Street Music Hall.

The circular tour is all but over. Close to where the Albert Clock towers over the area is the Corn Exchange, at the point where Corporation Street meets Victoria Street. Housed at No. 20 is the Victoria Hall, and along its length is a large space for circus performances.

Complete the journey by walking away from the Albert Clock southwards towards Cromac Street. Continue to Chichester Street and round the corner towards White Linen Hall, passing the National Equestrian Centre and the magnificent hall that houses Batty's Circus.

If it is the right day, 'Blondin, the Hero of Niagra' will be performing in the grounds. Turning left and walking straight ahead for 100 yards will finish the tour at the Ulster Hall.

Extras

Encore

I have included some music hall song lyrics, some of the 'big hits', for your interest.

I loved her and she might have been
The happiest in the land,
But she fancied a foreigner
Who played the flageolet
In the middle of a German band.

Arthur Lloyd (1839-1904)

There I was waiting at the church
Waiting at the church, waiting at the church
When I found he'd left me in the lurch
Lor' how it did upset me.
All at once, he sent me round a note.
Here's the very note,
This is what he wrote:
Can't get away to marry you today,
My wife won't let me.

Vesta Tilley (1873-1951)

My name is McNamara
I'm the leader of the band
And tho' we're small in number
We're the best in all the land.
I am the conductor and
We often have to play
With all the best musicians
You hear about today.
. . . .
A credit to old Ireland,
Is McNamara's band.

Written by John J. Stamford for W.J. Ashcroft.

My old man said 'Follow the van,
And don't dilly-dally on the way!'
Off went the cart with the home packed on it,
I walked behind with my old cock linnet.
But I dillied and dallied, dallied and dillied,
Lost the van and don't know where to roam.
You can't trust the 'specials' like the old time coppers,
When you can't find your way home.

Marie Lloyd (1870-1922)

Hello! Hello! Who's your lady friend?
Who's the little girlie by your side?
I've seen you with a girl or two,
Oh, oh, oh I am surprised at you!
Hello! Hello! Stop your little games,
Don't you think your ways ought to mend?
It isn't the girl I saw you with at Brighton,
Who, who, who's your lady friend?

Harry Frayson (1869-1913)

There's an old mill by the stream, Nellie Dean,
Where we used to sit and dream, Nellie Dean,
And the waters as they flow,
Seem to murmur sweet and low,
You've my heart's desire,
I love you Nellie Dean.

Gertie Gitana (1887-1957)

As I walk along the Bois Bou-long
With an independent air, you can hear the girls declare,
'He must be a millionaire.'
You can hear them sigh, and wish to die,
You can see them wink the other eye,
At the man who broke the bank at Monte Carlo.

Charles Coborn (1852-1945)

Come, come, come and make eyes at me
Down at the old Bull and Bush
Come, come, have some port wine with me
Down at the old Bull and Bush.
Here's the little German band,
Just let me hold your hand, dear,
Do! Do! Come and have a drink or two,
Down at the old Bull and Bush.

Florrie Forde (1876-1940)

We've been together now for forty years
And it don't seem a day too much.
Oh there ain't a lady living in the land,
As I'd swap for my dear, old Dutch.
No, there ain't a lady living in the land,
That I'd swap for my dear old Dutch.

Albert Chevalier (1866-1942)

I'm Henry the Eighth I am,
Henry the Eighth I am, I am.
I got married to the widow next door,
She's been married seven times before.
Every one was a Henry,
She wouldn't have a Willie or a Sam.
I'm her eighth old man named Henry.
Henry the Eighth I am.

Harry Campion (1866-1942)

I belong to Glasgow,
Dear old Glasgow town.
There's something the matter with Glasgow,
For it's going round and round.
I'm only a common, old working chap,
As anyone can see.
But when I get a drink on a Saturday,
Glasgow belongs to me.

Will Fyffe (1855-1944)

Roamin' in the gloamin',
On the bonny banks of Clyde,
Roamin' in the gloamin',
With a lassie by my side,
When the sun has gone to rest,
That's the time that we love best.
Oh, it's lovely roamin' in the gloamin'.

Sir Harry Lander (1870-1950)

Oh, I do like to be beside the seaside,
I do like to be beside the sea.
I do like to stroll along the prom, prom, prom,
Where the brass band plays Tiddley om pom pom.

Mark Sheridan (1865-1918)

Albert
Chevalier
(Mander &
Mitchenson,
1965).

I'm twenty-one today,
I'm twenty-one today,
I got the key of the door,
Never been twenty-one before.
And Pa says I can do what I like,
So that's hip, hip, hooray.
He's a jolly good fellow,
Twenty-one today.

Jack Pleasants (1874-1923)

He'd fly through the air with the greatest of ease,
A daring young man on the flying trapeze.
His movements were graceful. All the girls he could please,
And my love he purloined away.

George Leybourne (1842-1884

Daddy wouldn't buy me a bow-wow,
Daddy wouldn't buy me a bow-wow,
I've got a little cat, I am very fond of that,
But I'd rather have a bow-wow-wow.

Vesta Victoria (1873-1951)

Will Fyffe
(Mander &
Mitchenson,
1965).

(She was as) beautiful as a butterfly
And as proud as a queen,
Was pretty little Polly Perkins,
Of Paddington Greens.

                    Harry Clifton (1832-1872)

Daisy, Daisy give me your answer, do!
I'm half-crazy, all for the love of you!
It won't be a stylish marriage.
I can't afford a carriage.
But you'll look sweet on the seat,
Of a bicycle built for two.

                    Katie Lawrence (?-1912/13)

She's my lady love,
She is my dove, my baby love.
She's no girl for sitting down to dream.
She's the only queen Laguna knows.
I know she likes me,
I know she likes me,
Because she says so.

Vesta Tilley (Mander & Mitchenson, 1965).

She is the lily of Laguna,
She is my lily and my rose.

Eugene Stratton (1861–1918)

The Amusement's Column

This is a list of music halls, theatres and other buildings, used for entertainment in Belfast, that appeared in the Amusement's Column of various newspapers across three centuries. They are listed in chronological order.

The Market House	High Street	1639–1810
The Vaults	Weigh House Lane	1749–1769
The Mill Gate	Millfield	1768–1788
The Exchange / Assembly Rooms	2 Waring Street	1769– ?
Little Theatre, Donegall Arms	High Street	1778– ?

New Theatre	Ann Street	1778–1792
Theatre / Theatre Royal	Arthur Square	1793–1915
North Street Theatre	North Street	early 1800s
Commercial Buildings	1–3 Waring Street	1819– ?
New Harmonic Saloon	Castle Lane	1832– ?
The Music Hall	May Street	1840–1872
The Shakespeare	Castle Lane	1841–1870
Robert Burns Tavern & Concert Room	Long Lane	1846–1858
Oddfellows Hall	North Street	1847–1852
Hibernian Theatre OR the Royal Hibernian Concert Hall	Smithfield Square	1849–1858
National Theatre	Smithfield Square	1849–1863
The Corn Exchange	Corporation Street	1851– ?
The Star Concert Rooms / Alhambra Concert Rooms	21 Ann Street	1852–1868
Victoria Hall	Victoria Street	1854–1890
McCormick's Theatre	Smithfield Square	1860s
The Theatre	Lodge Road	1860s
Ulster Hall	Dublin Road	1862– ?
The Imperial Colosseum	Police Square	1861–1875
Colosseum / New Colosseum / Colosseum Hotel	Victoria Square	1875–1881
Royal Alhambra Theatre of Varieties	North Street	1871–1959
Traverse's Musical Lounge	Victoria Square	1879
Great George's Street Music Hall	Great George's Street	1880–1885
St George's Hall	High Street	1882–1908
Buffalo Variety Theatre	Victoria Square	1882–1889
Bijou Empire	Victoria Square	1891–1892
Olympia Palace	Glengall Place	1891–1894
The Star Music Hall / The Office	Church Street	1892–1908
Empire Theatre of Varieties (1)	Victoria Square	1892
Empire Theatre of Varieties (2)	Victoria Square	1894–1961
Grand Opera House	Great Victoria Street	1895
Palace of Varieties	Great Victoria Street	1904–1909
The Royal Hippodrome	Great Victoria Street	1907–1961
The Alexandra / Palladium	Grosvenor Road	1911–1914
The Coliseum (cine-variety)	Grosvenor Road	1914–1959
The Gaiety (cine-variety)	Upper North Street	1916–1956

From 1910 there were numerous 'cine-variety' picture houses, among them the Popular (Lower Newtownard's Road); the Palace (York Street) and the Princess Picture Palace (Newtownard's Road).

Belfast's Early Pub Scene

The music brought into the inns and taverns by singers and instrumentalists, and the ballads, told and retold by storytellers, laid the foundation for music hall. Belfast was no exception, where there seemed to be a pub on every corner and several in between, as in Smithfield Square.

Of the many pubs in the town's centre, I have chosen a selection ranging across the centuries. Some names will be familiar and some won't be. The first-known date is stated.

1612	Sir Moses Cellars	St George's Parish Church area
1630	White's Tavern	Wine cellar entry, Lombard St
17th Century	Thatch House Tavern	Waring St / Bridge St Corner
1750	Dr Franklin's Tavern	Sugar House Lane (Church St)
1811	Haylock's Tavern	destroyed 1941
1654	Widow Partridge's Inn	location unknown
1690	Eagle & Child	location unknown
1719	Adam & Eve	location unknown
1720	Kelly's Cellars	Bank Street (still there)
1738	George Inn	North Street
1739	Angel & Two Bibles	Bridge Street
1739	Race Horse	North Street
1750	Madden's Bar	Smithfield
1756	Cross Guns	High Street, facing Cornmarket
1768	Pewter Plates	Bridge Street
1791	Crown Tavern	High Street, Crown entry
1808	The Monkey Sharing the Goat	location unknown
1810	Garrick Bar	Chichester Street
1813	Hounds and Hare	North Street
1819	White Cross Inn	Garfield / North Street corner
1820	Morning Star	Pottinger's Entry (still there)
1835	Royal Bar	Sandy Row
1839	Crown Bar	Great Victoria Street
1840	The Washington	Howard Street
1859	The Kitchen Bar	Victoria Square

I'll call 'time' there, for the list is endless and I wanted to highlight those of the early years, when theatre and music hall in Belfast were developing and growing.

Recommended CDs

Here are some suggestions in case the song lyrics above do not satisfy:

Golden Years of Music Hall
On the Halls
Your Own, Your Very Own
Glory of Music Halls (Volume 2)

Bibliography

Bardon, Jonathan. *Belfast – An Illustrated History* (Belfast: Blackstaff Press, 1982)

Baker, Richard Anthony. *British Music Hall – An Illustrated History* (Stroud: Sutton Publishing Ltd, 2005)

Benn, George. *A History of the Town of Belfast – From Earliest Times to the Close of the Eighteenth Century* (London: Marcus Ward & Co. Ltd, 1877)

Brett, C.E.B. *Buildings of Belfast*, 2nd Edition (Belfast: Friars' Bush Press, 1985)

Brett, C.E.B. *Georgian Belfast 1750 – 1850* (Dublin: The Royal Irish Academy and Belfast National Historical & Philosophical Society, 2004)

Byrne, Ophelia. *The Stage in Ulster from the Eighteenth Century* (Belfast: Linen Hall Library, 1997)

Doherty, James. *Standing Room Only* (Belfast: Lagan Historical Society, 1997)

Findlater, Alex. *Findlater – The Story of a Dublin Merchant Family (1774 – 2001)* (Dublin: A&A Farmer, 2001)

Gaffikin, T. 'Belfast 50 Years Ago', *Belfast Newsletter* (Belfast: 1876)

Gallagher, Lyn. *The Grand Opera House.* (Belfast: Blackstaff Press, 1995)

Gammond, Peter. *Your Own, Your Very Own!* (London: Ian Allen Ltd, 1971)

Gillespie, Raymond & Royle, Stephen. A. *Irish Historical Towns – Belfast, Part 1 to 1840* (Dublin: Dublin University Press, 2003)

Gray, John. *Popular Entertainment – Belfast, the Making of a City* (Belfast: Appletree Press, 1983)

Lawrence, W.J. *Annals of the Old Belfast Stage 1731 – 1831*, Linen Hall Library, Belfast (Belfast: 1897)

Lawrence, W.J. *Old Theatres – Days & Ways* (London: Harrup & Co. Ltd, 1935)

Mander, Raymond & Mitchenson, Jon. *British Music Hall - A Story in Pictures.* (London: Studio Vista, 1965).

Maxwell, Constantina. *Dublin Under the Georges* (London: Faber & Faber, 1956)

McAllister, James. *A Belfast Chronicle – 1789* (Belfast: Friar's Bush Press, 1989)

Moore, Alfred S. *Old Belfast* (Belfast: Carter Publications, 1951)

O'Byrne, Cathal. *As I Roved Out* (Dublin: S.R. Publishers Ltd, 1946)

Open, Michael. *Fading Lights – Silver Screens* (Antrim: Greystone Press, 1985)

Patton, Marcus. *Central Belfast* (Belfast: Ulster Architectural Heritage Society, 1993)

Smyth, John. 'Octogenarian – Belfast 60 Years Ago', *Belfast Telegraph* (Belfast: 1868)

Young, R.M. *Historical Notes of Old Belfast* (Belfast: Marcus Ward & Co. Ltd, 1896)

The following were found in the Belfast Central Library newspaper film library:

Belfast Telegraph

Belfast Evening Telegraph

Belfast Morning News

Belfast WAIG

Ulster Saturday Night

Ireland Saturday Night

Belfast Newsletter

Belfast Evening News

Irish News

The Belfast Street Directories, courtesy of the Belfast Central Library and Public Records Office of Northern Ireland